W9-ABY-736

ROWAN UNIVERSITY
CAMPBELL LIBRARY
201 MULLICA HILL RD.
GLASSBORO, NJ 08028-1701

Microsoft® Access

Version 2002

Microsoft Office XP Application

plain & simple

Your fast-answers, no-jargon guide to Access 2002!

Curtis Frye

PUBLISHED BY
Microsoft Press
A Division of Microsoft Corporation
One Microsoft Way
Redmond, Washington 98052-6399

Copyright © 2001 by Curtis Frye

All rights reserved. No part of the contents of this book may be reproduced or transmitted in any form or by any means without the written permission of the publisher.

Library of Congress Cataloging-in-Publication Data
Frye, Curtis, 1968-
    Microsoft Access Version 2002 Plain & Simple / Curtis Frye.
        p. cm.
    Includes index.
    ISBN 0-7356-1454-7
    1. Microsoft Access.   2. Database management.   I. Title.

QA76.9.D3 F793 2001
005.75'65--dc21

2001044273

Printed and bound in the United States of America.

6 7 8 9   QWT   6 5

Distributed in Canada by H.B. Fenn and Company Ltd.

A CIP catalogue record for this book is available from the British Library.

Microsoft Press books are available through booksellers and distributors worldwide. For further information about international editions, contact your local Microsoft Corporation office or contact Microsoft Press International directly at fax (425) 936-7329. Visit our Web site at www.microsoft.com/mspress. Send comments to *mspinput@microsoft.com*.

FrontPage, Microsoft, Microsoft Press, the Office logo, Outlook, PivotChart, PivotTable, PowerPoint, Windows, and the Windows logo are either registered trademarks or trademarks of Microsoft Corporation in the United States and/or other countries. Other product and company names mentioned herein may be the trademarks of their respective owners.

The example companies, organizations, products, domain names, e-mail addresses, logos, people, places, and events depicted herein are fictitious. No association with any real company, organization, product, domain name, e-mail address, logo, person, place, or event is intended or should be inferred.

Acquisitions Editor: Kong Cheung
Project Editor: Kristen Weatherby
Technical Editor: LJ Locher

Body Part No. X08-24418

3 3001 00905 253 0

For my twin.

Contents

4 Creating a Database   31

5 Customizing Fields   43

9 Creating Reports 99

10 Beautifying Forms and Reports 117

14 Customizing Access · 185

15 Presenting Table and Query Data Dynamically · 203

i Index · 217

Acknowledgments

I shouldn't say this, but writing *Microsoft Access Version 2002 Plain & Simple* was probably the easiest part of the project. Kristen Weatherby was both project editor and copy editor, and her ability to manage this project and several others without losing her sense of humor was vital to getting the book out on time. LJ Locher was everything I could have asked for in a technical editor; she caught both of my mistakes, added valuable insights throughout the book, and was a joy to work with. Rob Nance, the principal artist on this book, was instrumental in guiding Paula Gorelick, the book's compositor, in laying out the screens and task steps so that they made sense. I'd like to thank them both for their admirable work. I'd also like to thank Lisa Pawlewicz for her reliable proofreading, and Shane-Armstrong Information Systems for developing the index.

Thanks as well to Kong Cheung, who invited me back for a second solo book with Microsoft Press; my agent, Neil Salkind of StudioB; and David and Sherry Rogelberg, the founders of StudioB, who showed faith in my potential as a writer so many years ago.

About This Book

I f you want to get the most from your computer and your software with the least amount of time and effort—and who doesn't?—this book is for you. You'll find *Microsoft Access Version 2002 Plain & Simple* to be a straightforward, easy-to-read reference tool. With the premise that your computer should work for you, not you for it, this book's purpose is to help you get your work done quickly and efficiently so that you can get away from the computer and live your life.

No Computerese!

Let's face it—when there's a task you don't know how to do but you need to get it done in a hurry, or when you're stuck in the middle of a task and can't figure out what to do next, there's nothing more frustrating than having to read page after page of technical background material. You want the information you need—nothing more, nothing less—and you want it now! *And* it should be easy to find and understand.

That's what this book is all about. It's written in plain English—no technical jargon and no computerese. There's no single task in the book that takes more than two pages. Just look the task up in the index or the table of contents, turn to the page, and there's the information you need, laid out in an illustrated, step-by-step format. You don't get bogged down by the whys and wherefores: just follow the steps and get your work done with a minimum of hassle.

Occasionally you might have to turn to another page if the procedure you're working on is accompanied by a "See Also." That's because there's a lot of overlap among tasks, and we didn't want to keep repeating ourselves. We've scattered some useful Tips here and there, and thrown in a "Try This" or a "Caution" once in a while, but by and large we've tried to remain true to the heart and soul of the book, which is that the information you need should be available to you at a glance.

Useful Tasks...

Whether you use Access at home or on the road, we've tried to pack this book with procedures for everything we could think of that you might want to do, from the simplest tasks to some of the more esoteric ones.

...And the Easiest Way to Do Them

Another thing we've tried to do in this book is find and document the easiest way to accomplish a task. Access often provides a multitude of methods to accomplish a single end result—which can be daunting or delightful, depending on the way you like to work. If you tend to stick with one favorite and familiar approach, we think the methods described in this book are the way to go. If you like trying out alternative techniques, go ahead! The intuitiveness of Access invites exploration, and you're likely to discover ways of doing things that you think are easier or that you like better than ours. If you do, that's great! It's exactly what the developers of Access had in mind when they provided so many alternatives.

A Quick Overview

Your computer probably came with Access preinstalled, but if you do have to install it yourself, the Setup Wizard makes installation so simple that you won't need our help anyway. So, unlike many computer books, this one doesn't start with installation instructions and a list of system requirements.

Next, you don't have to read this book in any particular order. It's designed so that you can jump in, get the information you need, and then close the book and keep it near your computer until the next time you need to know how to get something done. But that doesn't mean we scattered the information about with wild abandon. We've organized the book so that the tasks you want to accomplish are arranged in two levels—you'll find the overall type of task you're looking for under a main section title such as "Creating a New Database," "Getting Help," "Exporting Data to Other Programs," and so on. Then, in each of those sections, the smaller tasks within the main task are arranged in a loose progression from the simplest to the more complex.

Sections 2, 3, and 4 cover the basics: starting Access and shutting it down, sizing and arranging program windows, getting help from within the program and on the Web, what types of objects are available in an Access database, and the role each of those objects fulfills. There's also a lot of useful information about designing and creating a new database, either from scratch or with the help of Access; navigating within a database; creating relationships between tables; and getting data from other Access databases. You'll also learn about what's new in Access 2002, including simpler ways to perform the most common tasks, better data recovery if your program crashes, and how to link your data to other data on the Web.

Section 5 is all about customizing your table fields—the different types of fields available to you; how to add, delete, and rearrange fields; and how to make data entry easier for you and your colleagues. You'll find the information helpful whether you want to change how a field displays its data, set a default value for a field, ensure the data entered into the field is appropriate for that field, and even let you and your colleagues enter table data by picking the proper value from a list.

Section 6 focuses on working with entire tables, rather than individual fields in a table. Here's where you'll find information about entering data quickly, finding and replacing table text, and modifying how Access displays your data in a table. There's also a short section here on filtering a table's contents, which lets you limit the data displayed to exactly what you need to make a decision.

Sections 7, 8, 9, and 10 are all about building database objects to take best advantage of your data—creating forms, which let you present your data in an attractive format and enter new table records; defining queries, which let you ask specific questions of your table data; building reports, which summarize your data and make it easy to create mailing labels; and changing the appearance of your forms and reports to make them more attractive or to conform with a company's color scheme. The possibilities are endless, and we know you'll be thrilled by the flexibility, power, and ease-of-use of the Access tools at your disposal.

Section 11 is about interacting with other programs, by including files created in other programs in your databases, adding pictures to forms and reports, or including Microsoft Excel charts in your database. You will also find out how to exchange data with other programs, whether that means exporting Access table or query data to another program or reading data from another program's files into Access.

The final sections, 12 through 15, deal with more advanced topics: sharing database data on the Web; administering your database so you can, if necessary, identify the data that is open for anyone to look over and separate that data from tables or queries that might contain more sensitive information; setting up switchboards that make your databases easier to move around in; customizing Access by changing the items that show up on the program's toolbar and menus; creating macros that automate repetitive or lengthy tasks; creating forms that let you dynamically reorganize your data; and diagnosing and taking care of problems. If you think these tasks sound complex, rest assured that they're not—Access makes them so easy that you'll sail right through them.

A Few Assumptions

We had to make a few educated guesses about you, our audience, when we started writing this book. Perhaps you just use Access for personal reasons—keeping track of your books, music, contacts, and so on. Perhaps you use Access at work to maintain records of your inventory, customers, and the orders they place. Or maybe

you run a small home-based business. Taking all these possibilities into account, we assumed that you'd need to know how to create, modify, and work with all of the basic Access database objects; to administer the database; and to share the data on the Internet or over your company's internal network.

Another assumption we made is that—initially, anyway—you'd use Access just as it came, meaning that you'd leave the menus and toolbars as they were when you installed the program. If you want to change the toolbars and menus, you can certainly do so by following the instructions in "Modifying Toolbars" on page 186 and "Modifying Menus" on page 188. However, because our working style is somewhat traditional, and because Access is set up to work in the traditional style, that's what we've described in the procedures and graphics throughout this book.

A Final Word (or Two)

We had three goals in writing this book:

- Whatever you want to do, we want the book to help you get it done.

- We want the book to help you discover how to do things you *didn't* know you wanted to do.

- And, finally, if we've achieved the first two goals, we'll be well on the way to the third, which is for our book to help you *enjoy* using Access. We think that's the best gift we could give you to thank you for buying our book.

We hope you'll have as much fun using *Microsoft Access Version 2002 Plain & Simple* as we've had writing it. The best way to learn is by *doing,* and that's how we hope you'll use this book. Jump right in!

2 Introducing Microsoft Access 2002

✳ NEW FEATURE

Microsoft Access 2002 is designed to help you store, combine, and ask questions of large collections of data relevant to your business or your home life. You can create databases to track products and sales for a garden supply company, or, just as easily, build databases to keep track of your books and holiday card lists. Regardless of the specific use you have in mind, Access is a versatile program you can use to store and retrieve data quickly.

Working with Access is pretty straightforward. The program has a number of wizards (step-by-step processes) you can use to create entire databases, or just parts of them. You also have the freedom to create databases and their components from scratch, giving you the flexibility you need to build any database you need.

This section of the book covers the basics: what a database is and how it works, starting Access, shutting it down, opening databases, and the new features you'll find in Access 2002. There's also an overall view of the Access window, with labels for the most important parts of the program. You can use that image as a touchstone for learning more about Access.

Introducing Databases

Storing Data on Index Cards

Before computers came along, one popular way of storing data was on index cards. If you ran a gardening supply store, you could keep track of your products by creating a card for each product, dividing the cards into product categories, and then alphabetizing the cards in each section by product name. Each card would have relevant data like the product's name, unique identifier, category, price, description, and the supplier's name and phone number.

```
FN1001

FURNITURE              GARDEN SUPPLY CO.

TWO-PERSON BENCH       (425) 555-0102

$179.95

BLONDE ASH WITH A TRANSPARENT

PRESERVATIVE COAT.
```

To find all of the products from a specific supplier, you'd either need to keep track of the products on a separate sheet of paper or go through the cards and pull every one representing a product made by that supplier.

Storing Data on the Computer

If you store the same data on the computer, however, you could find all of the products from a specific supplier much more easily. As an example, you might create a Microsoft Word table with a column for each type of data you want to store.

Category	Product ID	Product Name	Price	Supplier	Phone
Tools	TL2248	Garden Hose (50')	$28.00	All Gardening Needs	4255550102
Tools	TL2697	Gardener's Rake	$18.95	All Gardening Needs	4255550102
Tools	TL2539	Grafting Knife	$18.95	Sharp Implements	4255550035
Tools	TL2538	Grafting/Splicing Tool	$57.95	Sharp Implements	4255550035
Tools	TL1182	Holster	$10.00	Leather Goods	4255550168
Tools	TL0802	Long-handled Loppers	$64.95	Sharp Implements	4255550035
Tools	TL0038	Nutcracker	$18.00	Home Goods	4255550047
Tools	TL1549	Overhead Loppers	$69.95	Sharp Implements	4255550035
Tools	TL3001	Pruners, Left-handed	$54.00	Sharp Implements	4255550035
Tools	TL3002	Pruners, Right-handed	$54.00	Sharp Implements	4255550035
Tools	TL0460	Pruning Saw	$19.95	Sharp Implements	4255550035
Tools	TL3898	Saw	$34.95	Sharp Implements	4255550035
Tools	TL4281	Sharpener	$14.95	Sharp Implements	4255550035
Tools	TL1133	Timer, Greenhouse	$44.95	Home Goods	4255550047
Tools	TL0210	Timer, Watering	$44.95	Home Goods	4255550047

With the list in a Word table, you could change the order of the table rows to group all of the products from one supplier together...all you'd need to do then is scroll down through the table until you found the products from the supplier you wanted.

Using Word to store your data isn't the best solution, however. One limitation is that there's no way to combine information from two tables, so you need to write the supplier's phone number in every row representing a product from that supplier. If that phone number changed, you'd need to change the phone number entry in every table row representing a product from that supplier.

Storing Data in a Database

Databases, by contrast, are designed to combine data from several sources into a single table. Once data is entered into a table, it can be combined with other tables in the database to produce valuable information. It's possible, for example, to store information about suppliers in one table and information about products in another table. If a supplier changed its phone number, you'd only need to change the phone number once.

Information about a supplier

Supplier ID	Company Name	Contact Name	
1	Exotic Liquids	Charlotte Cooper	Pu
2	New Orleans Cajun Delights	Shelley Burke	Orc
3	Grandma Kelly's Homestead	Regina Murphy	Sal

Product ID	Product Name	Category	Quantity Pe
6	Grandma's Boysenberry Spread	Condiments	12 - 8 oz jars
7	Uncle Bob's Organic Dried Pears	Produce	12 - 1 lb pkgs.
8	Northwoods Cranberry Sauce	Condiments	12 - 12 oz jars
(AutoNumber)			

Information about each product is listed on a separate row.

New in Access 2002

Access 2002 has a number of new features that make it easier to maintain and manipulate data in your databases. New features are marked throughout the book with the new icon ⊛ **NEW FEATURE**, but there are two neat new features you should know about from the start.

Crash Recovery ⊛ NEW FEATURE

If you're running Access and the power goes out, Access won't have time to save your work and close the program gracefully. The next time you run Access, however, the program will look for files that weren't saved properly. Any files the program finds will be displayed in the Recovery pane, at the left edge of the Access window. You can open the file by clicking its name—Access will recover as much of the data from the file as it can. In many cases, all of your work will have been recovered. If not, you will still have all of your work from the last time you saved.

The Task Panes ⊛ NEW FEATURE

When you start Access, the task pane appears at the right edge of the Access window. The task pane contains hyperlinks to a number of common tasks, such as opening or creating a database, pasting information from a clipboard, or searching for specific text.

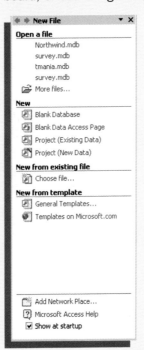

The first task pane you see, the New File task pane, is actually one of three—the other two are the Clipboard and Search task panes. The Clipboard task pane keeps track of any items you've copied to the system clipboard and makes them available to you with a single mouse click.

The Search task pane lets you look for files with specific names or content on your computer.

Running Access

Once you've installed Access on your computer, you can run it to create new databases or to work with existing databases. There are several ways to run Access—you can run it from the Start menu or by double-clicking a shortcut on your desktop.

Start Access

① Click the Start button on the Task bar.

② Point to Programs.

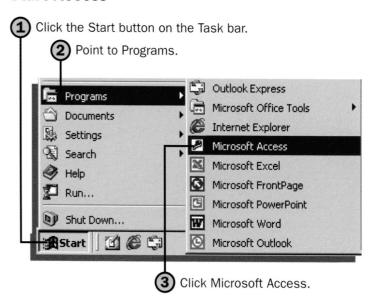

③ Click Microsoft Access.

> ⚠ **TIP: To see the list of available task panes, click the down arrow on the task pane's title bar.**

Create a Shortcut for Access

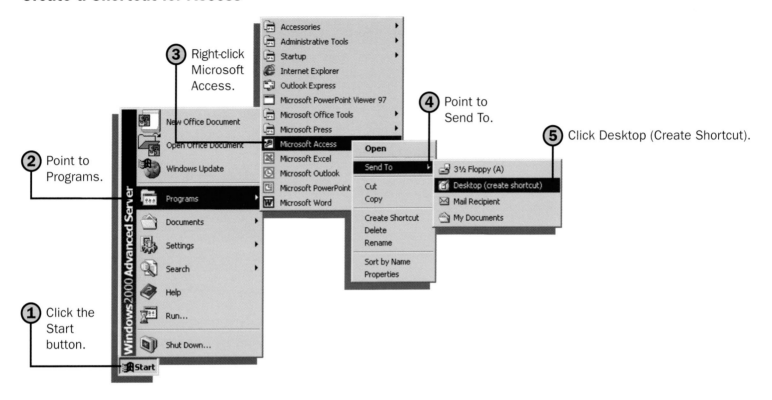

Right-click Microsoft Access.

Point to Send To.

Click Desktop (Create Shortcut).

Point to Programs.

Click the Start button.

! **TIP:** You can rename a shortcut by right-clicking it, choosing Rename from the shortcut menu that appears, and then typing the shortcut's new name.

Surveying the Access Window

- The Title bar displays the name of the database and the window control buttons.

- The Menu bar holds groups of related commands. The exact commands available change based on your position in the database.

- The task pane lets you perform common tasks with one mouse click.

- The Database toolbar has buttons you can click to save your work, print the current object, copy or paste items, and perform many other useful tasks.

- The Status bar indicates the progress of any ongoing processes.

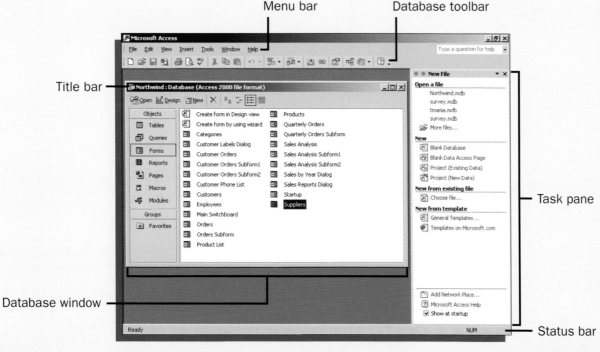

Opening a Database

When you start Access, the task pane appears on the right side of the Access window. A list of recently opened files appears at the top of the task pane, in the Open A File section. You can pick the file you want to open from the list that appears or, if the file you want isn't on that list, click More Files to display the Open dialog box. From the Open dialog box, you can navigate to the directory containing the database you want to open.

Open a Database on Startup

1 Click the Start button, point to Programs, and then click Microsoft Access.

2 Click More Files.

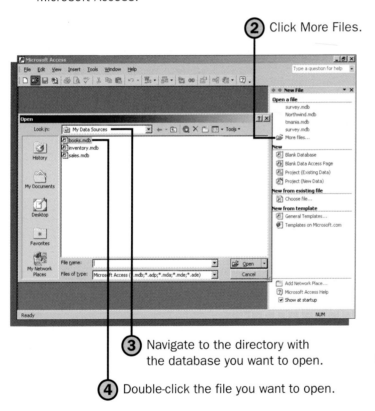

3 Navigate to the directory with the database you want to open.

4 Double-click the file you want to open.

Open a Recently Used Database

1 Click the Start button, point to Programs, and then click Microsoft Access.

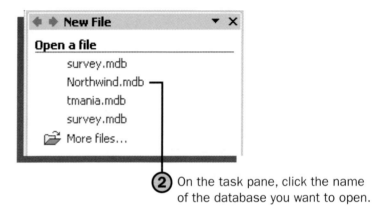

2 On the task pane, click the name of the database you want to open.

> **!** TIP: If the task pane doesn't appear, you can display the Open dialog box by clicking the Open button on the Database toolbar.

> **TRY THIS:** Open any database, choose the Options command from the Tools menu, click the General tab, type 4 in the Recently used file list box, and then click OK.

Sizing and Arranging Windows

You work with windows in the Access program the same way you work with windows on your desktop. You can make a database object's window as large as the Access window itself; if you have more than one object open at a time, you can choose from several display arrangements to order the windows most effectively.

Resize a Window

● Click the Maximize button to make the window take up the entire Access window.

● Click the Minimize button to represent the window as a Title bar at the bottom of the Access window.

● Click the Restore button to return the window to its previous size.

● Drag the left or right border of the window to resize it horizontally.

● Drag the top or bottom border of the window to resize it vertically.

● Drag a corner to resize the window both horizontally and vertically.

● Drag the window's Title bar to change its position.

Title bar

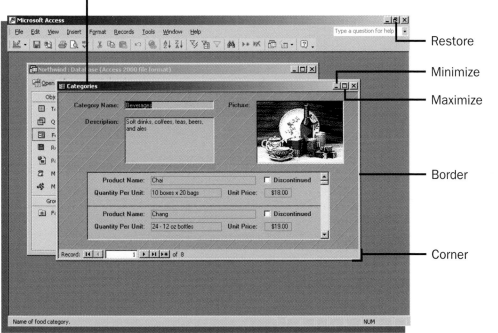

Restore

Minimize

Maximize

Border

Corner

> **TIP: Double-clicking a window's Title bar will maximize the window.**

> **CAUTION: If the Access window is smaller than the screen (that is, not maximized), it is possible for the Title bars of open objects to be positioned beyond the edge of the database window. If you think you've opened an object but don't see its title, maximize the database window to show all open objects.**

Arrange Windows

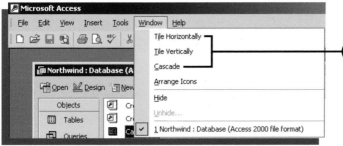

1 Choose the desired arrangement from the Window menu.

> **!** TIP: You can hide a window without closing it by clicking the window's Title bar and then choosing Hide from the Window menu. To redisplay the window, choose Unhide from the Window menu, click the name of the window to unhide, and then click OK.

Closing a Database and Exiting Access

When you're done working with an Access database, you should close it to free up system resources and let your computer run other programs more quickly. By the same token, once you've completed all the work you need to do in Access you should exit the program entirely.

Close a Database

1 Click the Close box.

> **!** TIP: If you're done working with the current database and want to open another, save your work and then click the Open button on the standard toolbar.

> **✋** CAUTION: Clicking the Close box at the top right of the Access window will exit Access, not just close the active database.

Exit Access

1 Choose Exit from the File menu.

Getting Help

There are lots of ways to get help while you're using Access. If there's something specific you want to do and you can't find it in this book, unlikely though that is, you can get help by asking a question, browsing through the range of Help files available in Access, or by going to the Web.

Get Help Using the Ask A Question Box

① Type your question in the Ask A Question Box, and then press Enter.

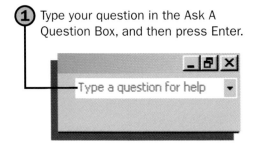

② Click the topic you want to view.

> **TRY THIS: Type** What's New **in the Ask a Question Box, press Enter, and then click What's New In Microsoft Access.**

Get Help Using Microsoft Access Help

① Choose Microsoft Access Help from the Help menu.

② Click the Contents tab.

③ Double-click the categories until a list of help topics appears.

④ Double-click the help topic you want to display.

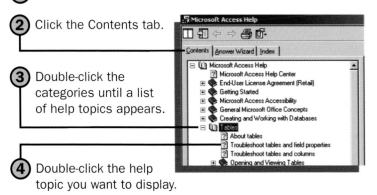

Get Help on the Web

① Choose Office On The Web from the Help menu.

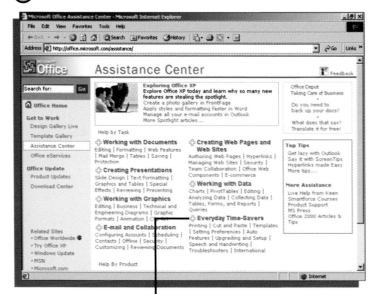

② Follow the hyperlinks on the Microsoft Office Assistance Center Web site to find the topic you want.

> **TIP: You can visit the Microsoft Office Assistance Center site directly by opening your Web browser and typing** http://office.microsoft.com/assistance/ **in the Address box.**

Printing Database Objects

Whether it's to create handouts for a meeting, include your Access data in a written report, or make a paper copy of a form for easy reference, you will probably want to print all or part of your data at some point. The easiest way to print an object (and all of the data it contains) is to click the Print button on the Standard toolbar, but you can also choose to have much more control over which data you print and how it will appear on the page.

Print an Object

② Click the Print button.

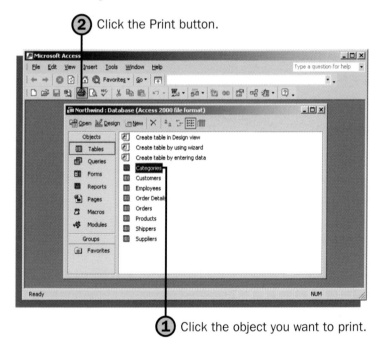

① Click the object you want to print.

Print Selected Pages

② Choose Print from the File menu.

① Click the object you want to print.

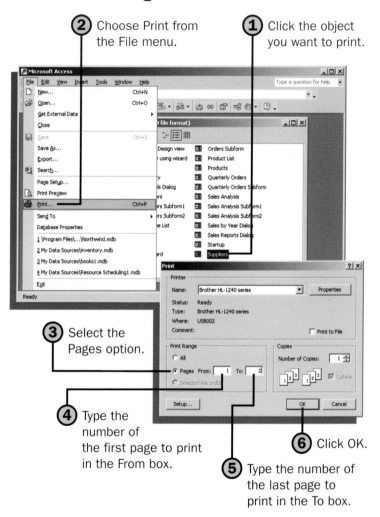

③ Select the Pages option.

④ Type the number of the first page to print in the From box.

⑤ Type the number of the last page to print in the To box.

⑥ Click OK.

> ⚠ TIP: To print a single page (such as page 3), put the page number in both the From and To boxes. In this case, you would print "From 3 To 3".

Print Selected Records

(1) Click the Tables button.   **(2)** Double-click the table with the records you want to print.

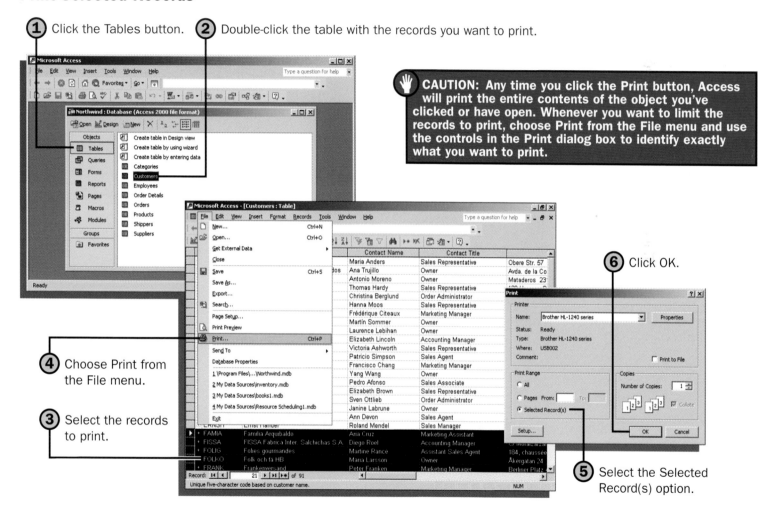

CAUTION: Any time you click the Print button, Access will print the entire contents of the object you've clicked or have open. Whenever you want to limit the records to print, choose Print from the File menu and use the controls in the Print dialog box to identify exactly what you want to print.

(6) Click OK.

(4) Choose Print from the File menu.

(3) Select the records to print.

(5) Select the Selected Record(s) option.

Getting to Know Access Databases

Microsoft Access is a powerful program with a wide variety of objects you can create to manage, locate, and present important information. The best way to get familiar with Access and what you can do with it is to dive right in by examining a sample database. Access 2002 comes with the Northwind sample database, which chronicles the activities and resources of a food and beverage dealer. In addition to the Northwind sample database, Access also has several database wizards you can use to create databases to track your books, contacts, or music collection.

Each object type has a definite role in the functioning of the database. Tables are the building block of your collection—that's where the data is stored. You can ask questions about your data by creating queries, present the data one record at a time in forms, or group records by their contents in reports. One type of form is the switchboard, which has controls you can click to open popular database objects, organizes your database contents onto switchboard pages, and can even let the user exit Access by clicking a form button.

This chapter introduces the database elements you'll use most often, explains the elements of each object type, and shows you how to create your own database using a wizard.

Viewing Sample Databases

One of the best ways to get a feel for using Access is to work with an existing database. The Northwind database, which you installed along with Access, is a complete database with tables, queries, reports, and forms you can examine to see what goes into a solid database design.

TRY THIS: Choose Small Icons from the View menu. Then point to Arrange Icons on the View menu, and click By Name. This view represents the objects in the database window as icons representing their object type and arranges them in alphabetical order by name.

Open a Sample Database

1 Point to Sample Databases on the Help menu.

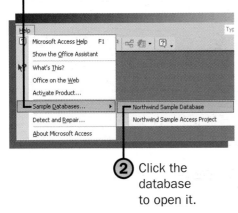

2 Click the database to open it.

TIP: You should open the Northwind Sample Database; the other sample file is meant to be used with another Microsoft database product.

Change Database View

1 Point to the desired view on the View menu.

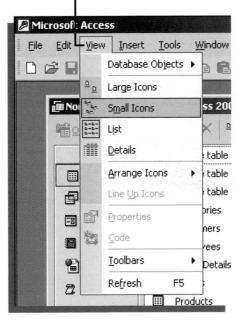

- Choose Large Icons if you want to represent the objects as full-size icons with the name of the object just below.

- Choose Small Icons if you want to represent the objects as smaller icons, with the name of the object just below.

- Choose List if you want to list the objects with the object's name to the right of the file.

- Choose Details to list the objects by name but with the object's size and the date it was last modified.

Working with Database Objects

Every element of a database, be it a table, form, report, or query, is represented in the Access window as an object. This section shows you how to display a category of objects, open an individual object for viewing, and open an object for editing; future sections will go into more detail about what you can do with each type of object.

Display a Class of Objects

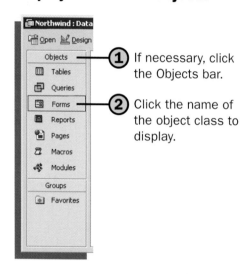

① If necessary, click the Objects bar.

② Click the name of the object class to display.

View an Object in Design View

① Click the target object.

② Click Design.

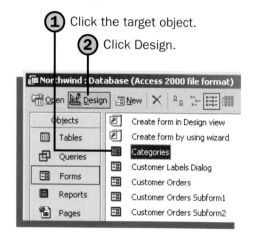

Delete an Object

① Click an object.

② Click the Delete button.

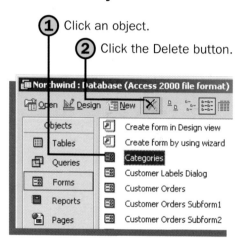

Open an Object

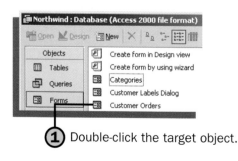

① Double-click the target object.

Save an Object

① Click the Save button.

Examining a Table

The basic building block of a database is the table, which is where you store your data. Tables are made up of columns (also called *fields*) and rows (also called *records*). A field holds a particular type of data, such as a name or phone number, while a record has a complete set of fields relating to an entity (such as a person's name, address, and phone number).

View a Table

① Click Tables on the Objects bar.

② Double-click a table.

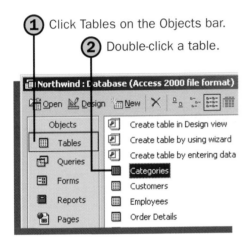

> **! TIP:** You can get a complete list of keyboard shortcuts in Access by typing keyboard shortcuts in the Ask A Question box and then clicking Keyboard Shortcuts from the list of topics that appears.

Navigate in a Table

- Press Tab to move to the next cell.

- Press Shift+Tab to move to the previous cell.

- Press Home to move to the first cell of the first row.

- Press End to move to the last cell of the active row.

- Drag the vertical scroll box up or down to view table rows not currently displayed.

- Drag the horizontal scroll box to the left or right to view fields not currently displayed.

- Use the controls on the record navigation bar to move among records.

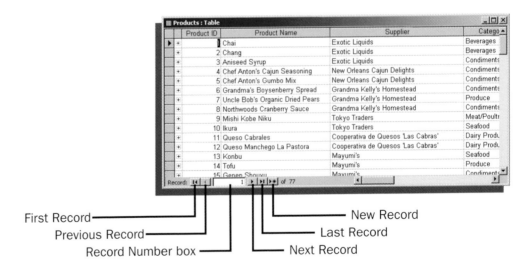

First Record

Previous Record

Record Number box

New Record

Last Record

Next Record

Examining a Form

Forms are database objects that make it easier for you to view data stored in tables or retrieved by queries. Rather than present the data in a compact grid, creating forms to display table and query data let you arrange fields on the form and add explanatory text to help you and your colleagues understand the form's contents. You can also enter new records into a table through a form.

> **CAUTION:** If you don't enter data in the last field, Access may not write your data to the table. You can save your work in progress by clicking the Save button on the Standard toolbar.

View a Form

1 If necessary, click Forms on the Objects bar.

2 Double-click a form.

> **TIP:** As in a table, you can use the navigation bar at the bottom left of the form window to move among the form records or, if the form is based on a table, to enter a new record.

Enter Data Using a Form

2 Type your data in the first field, and press Tab.

1 Click the New Record button.

3 Continue entering data. When you enter data in the last field and press Tab, Access will create a new record.

Navigating Using a Switchboard

When you create a database with a lot of tables, queries, and forms, it can be hard for your colleagues to recognize which objects hold which information. You can make their job easier by creating a switchboard with the most important objects on the front page. The usual name for the switchboard that appears when a database opens is "Main Switchboard."

Open a Switchboard

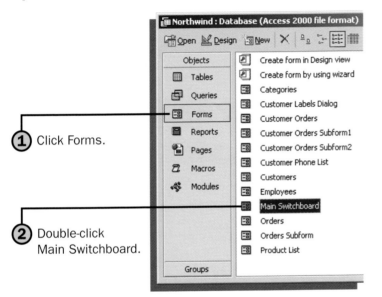

① Click Forms.

② Double-click Main Switchboard.

Move Using a Switchboard

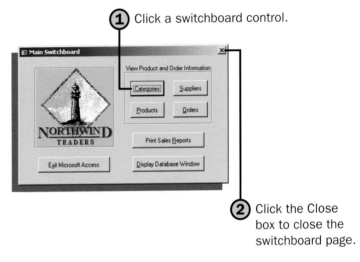

① Click a switchboard control.

② Click the Close box to close the switchboard page.

> SEE ALSO: For information about creating switchboards of your own, see "Creating a Switchboard" on page 180.

Examining a Query

When a table has just a few rows, it's easy to scroll through it for a few records with the data you want. For larger tables, though, you can create queries to find records that meet various criteria, like orders from a particular customer.

View a Query

1 If necessary, click Queries on the Objects bar.

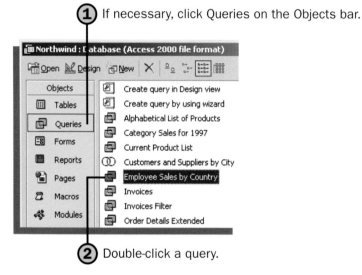

2 Double-click a query.

Examining a Report

Unlike forms, which show one record at a time, reports can show more than one record on the same page. The benefit of reports is that you can group the records a report displays to show all products in a given category before moving on to the products in the next category.

View a Report

1 If necessary, click Reports on the Objects bar.

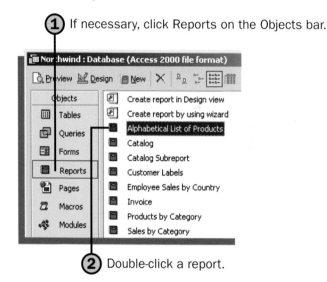

2 Double-click a report.

> **SEE ALSO:** For information about grouping records, see "Grouping Report Records" on page 111.

Creating a Database with the Database Wizard

Access comes with a number of templates you can use to create common databases, such as contact management, expense tracking, and tracking your and your colleagues' time and billing. Each template launches a wizard that steps you through the database creation process.

Create a Database with the Database Wizard

① Click the New button.

② Click General Templates.

⑤ Type the name of your database, and click Create.

⑥ Follow the instructions in the wizard.

⑦ Click Finish.

> **! TIP: Clicking Finish in any wizard screen accepts the default settings for the rest of the database elements.**

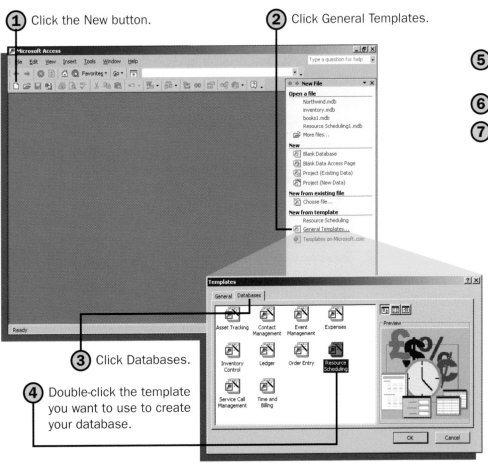

③ Click Databases.

④ Double-click the template you want to use to create your database.

Using the Database Wizards

Regardless of the type of database you want to create, you'll be asked to perform four tasks:

- Choose the tables and fields to put in the database.

- Choose a screen display style.

  The following graphics show the screens you'll be using.

- Choose a report style.

- Set a database name and graphic.

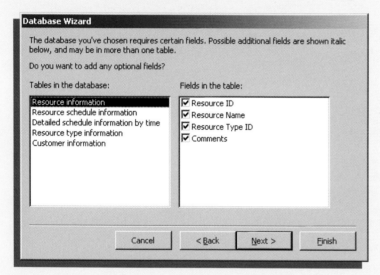

Choose a screen display style. You select a look for your database, which appears in the wizard screen's preview window.

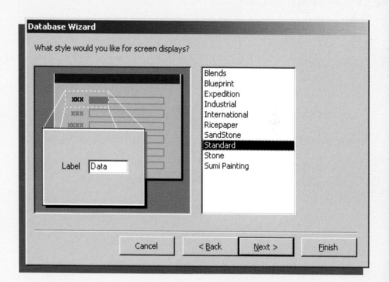

Choose a report style. On this screen, you choose how you want your database's reports to appear.

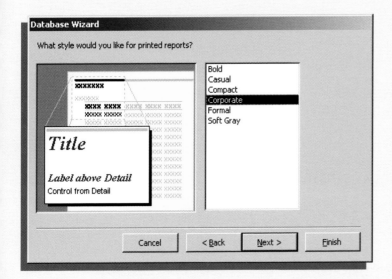

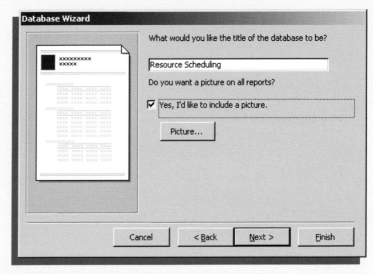

Set a database name and graphic. If you want to change the database's name from the default, you can type the new name in the screen's text box. You can also add a graphic to every report by selecting the Yes, I'd Like To Include A Picture check box, clicking Picture, and using the dialog box that appears to identify the picture to include.

Frequently Used Object Views

Each object has a number of *views*, or ways of looking at and working with the object and its contents. Opening any object in Design view, for example, lets you change the object's structure and appearance. The following table has a list of the most useful views available for each Access object type.

Object	Views	Description
Table	Design	Opens the table so you can add, delete, or modify fields.
	Datasheet	Displays the table data as rows in an unformatted worksheet.
Form	Design	Opens the form so you can add, delete, or modify fields and controls.
	Form	Displays the form data using the layout you created by hand or by wizard.
	Datasheet	Displays the form data as rows in an unformatted worksheet.
Report	Design	Opens the report so you can add, delete, or modify fields, controls, and grouping levels.
	Print Preview	Displays the report as it will be printed.
Query	Design	Opens the query so you can add, delete, or modify fields, criteria, and any actions the query takes when it runs.
	Datasheet	Displays the query results as rows in an unformatted worksheet.

4 Creating a Database

If none of the databases you can create using one of the Microsoft Access database wizards meets your needs, you can create a database from scratch. You're not totally on your own, though, as you can use the Table Wizard to build tables from existing models.

When you create a table using the Table Wizard, you'll see a list of model tables you can use to store information about your personal contacts or your books or music collection, or to record sales for your business. You can create a table with every suggested field, pick which fields you want, or even combine fields from more than one sample table.

Once you've created a table, whether from scratch or with the Table Wizard, you can change its structure as needed, such as by renaming an existing field or by adding an entirely new field to store additional data.

In this chapter, you'll learn how to:

● Design a database.

● Create a new database.

● Create tables with the Table Wizard.

● Create tables from scratch in Design view.

● Create and manage table relationships using key fields.

Designing a Database

The most basic object in a database is the table, where you store your data. You might be tempted to jam every type of data you want to store into a single table, but that's hardly ever the right way to design tables in a database. The following guidelines will help you create efficient tables.

One Table per Object

The first rule in creating database tables is to ensure that every table stores data about one type of object, whether that object is a person, a product, or an order. As an example, consider the Suppliers table from the Northwind database.

Suppliers : Table

Field Name	Data Type
SupplierID	AutoNumber
CompanyName	Text
ContactName	Text
ContactTitle	Text
Address	Text
City	Text
Region	Text
PostalCode	Text
Country	Text
Phone	Text
Fax	Text
HomePage	Hyperlink

This table has a field for everything you'd want to know about a supplier, with nothing extra. Consider this alternative design, which adds fields to describe the supplier's products.

Field Name	Data Type
SupplierID	AutoNumber
CompanyName	Text
ContactName	Text
ContactTitle	Text
Address	Text
City	Text
Region	Text
PostalCode	Text
Country	Text
Phone	Text
Fax	Text
HomePage	Hyperlink
ProductID	Text
ProductName	Text
Price	Currency

Aside from repeated data, deleting the record representing the last product from a supplier would remove all information about that supplier from your database. Rather than risk losing that information, it is much more efficient to create one table for the suppliers and another for the products.

Give Every Table a Primary Key

Another important consideration in creating a table is to assign a *primary key*. This field will contain a unique value that sets a record apart from all other records in the table. In the Northwind database's Shippers table, that role is filled by the ShipperID field.

Field Name	Data Type	Description
ShipperID	AutoNumber	Number automatically assigned to ne
CompanyName	Text	Name of shipping company.
Phone	Text	Phone number includes country code

Shippers : Table

It's also possible to create a primary key made up of more than one field, as in the Order Details table.

Field Name	Data Type	Description
OrderID	Number	Same as Order ID in Orders table.
ProductID	Number	Same as Product ID in Products table.
UnitPrice	Currency	
Quantity	Number	
Discount	Number	

Order Details : Table

The OrderID field identifies the order to which the item belongs, and the ProductID field identifies the product ordered.

Both fields are unique to this table and are needed to distinguish a record from all others because a single order might include more than one product and the same product might be included in more than one order.

Include Foreign Keys

A final way to make your tables more efficient is to include primary key fields from other tables, as with the SupplierID field in the Products table.

Field Name	Data Type	Description
ProductID	AutoNumber	Number automatically assigned to new product.
ProductName	Text	
SupplierID	Number	Same entry as in Suppliers table.
CategoryID	Number	Same entry as in Categories table.
QuantityPerUnit	Text	(e.g., 24-count case, 1-liter bottle).
UnitPrice	Currency	
UnitsInStock	Number	
UnitsOnOrder	Number	
ReorderLevel	Number	Minimum units to maintain in stock.
Discontinued	Yes/No	Yes means item is no longer available.

Products : Table

When a primary key from one table is stored in another table, it is called a *foreign key*. As you'll see later in this chapter, you can use foreign keys to create relationships between tables.

Creating a New Database

If you want to create a new database from scratch, you can do so by creating a blank database and then adding your own tables and other objects. You can also create a new database based on an existing database, saving yourself lots of time and effort.

Begin a New Database

① If necessary, click the New button to display the New File task pane.

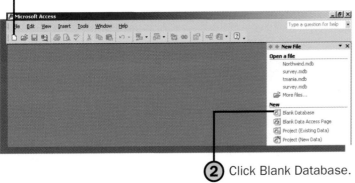

② Click Blank Database.

> **!** TIP: Access uses the name of the old database to name the new database. If the database you used as a base was named Contacts, the new database will be named Contacts 1. To rename the database, type the new name in the File Name box.

Create a New Database Based on Another Database

① If necessary, click the New button to display the New File task pane.

② Click Choose File.

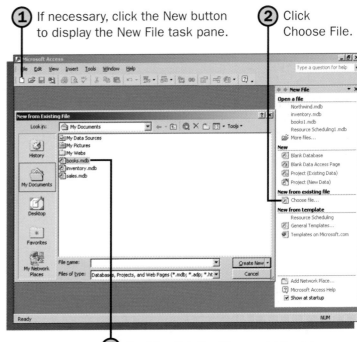

③ Double-click the file on which you want to base your new database.

Creating a Table with the Table Wizard

Rather than force you to create a new table from scratch when you start a new database, Access lets you use the Table Wizard to choose commonly used fields from a number of preconstructed tables.

TRY THIS: Double-click Create Table By Using Wizard, select the Personal option, click Books in the Sample Tables box, click the Add All button, click Next, and then click Finish to accept the table name "Books" and to create the table.

Step Through the Table Wizard

1 If necessary, click Tables on the Objects bar.

2 Double-click Create Table By Using Wizard.

3 Select a category of tables.

4 Click a table.

5 Click a field to add.

6 Click the Add button.

- To add every field in the Sample Fields box, click the Add All button.

- To remove a field from the table, click the field to remove and then click the Remove button.

- To remove all fields from the table, click the Remove All button.

7 Click Next to move to the next wizard page.

8 Type a name for your table.

9 Click Next to have the wizard set a primary key for you and move to the next wizard page.

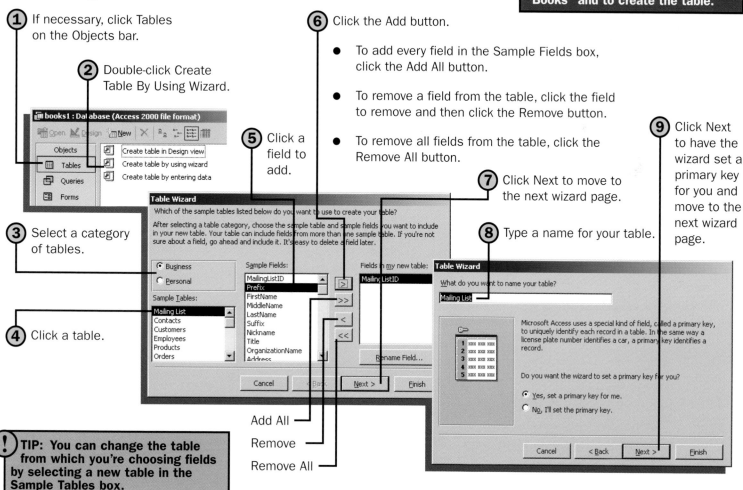

Add All

Remove

Remove All

TIP: You can change the table from which you're choosing fields by selecting a new table in the Sample Tables box.

Creating a Table in Design View

If you want to create a table without the benefit of any of the wizards available to you, you can do so by creating a new table and adding fields one at a time. Creating a table in Design view is a good way to become familiar with the table design tools at your disposal.

Build a Table in Design View

TIP: If you didn't assign a primary key, a dialog box appears asking you to do so.

① Click Tables on the Objects Bar.

② Double-click Create Table In Design View.

④ Click the down arrow in the Data Type box, click a data type for the field, and then press the Tab key.

⑤ Type a comment for the field in the Description box, and then press the Tab key to move to the next field.

③ Type a name for the first field in the Field Name box, and then press the Tab key.

⑥ When you are done adding fields, click Close.

⑦ Click Yes to save your work.

⑧ Type a name for the table in the Table Name box.

⑨ Click OK.

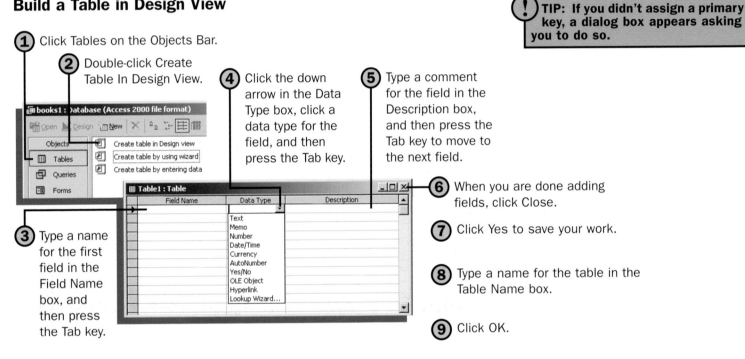

SEE ALSO: For more information about editing tables in Design view, see Chapter 5, "Customizing Fields."

Setting a Primary Key

One aspect of sound table design is to have a field (or group of fields) with a value unique for each row in the table. The fields that have the unique value are called the *primary key* field(s).

Assign a Primary Key

① If necessary, click Tables on the Objects Bar.

② Click a table.

③ Click Design.

⑥ Click the Save button to save your work.

⑤ Click the Primary Key button on the Table Design toolbar.

⑦ Click the Close box.

④ Click the row selector of the field to be the primary key.

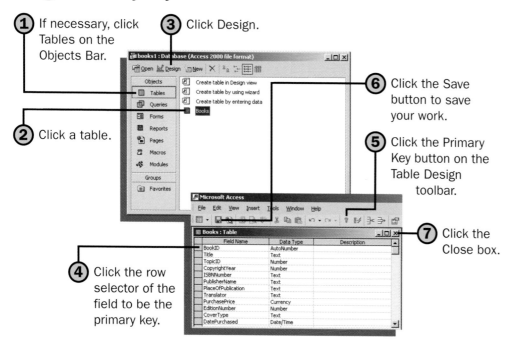

TIP: You can create a multiple-field primary key by Ctrl-clicking the row selectors of the fields to be in the primary key.

CAUTION: Be sure your primary field doesn't do double duty. The field's job is to distinguish a record from all other records in the same table and should contain a unique value, preferably one generated by Access. Leave it to the other fields to store names, addresses, phone numbers, and the like.

Getting Data from Other Access Tables

Many times you'll find that data from another database would be nice to have in the database you're working on. You can bring tables (or other objects) into your database using the File menu's Import command.

Copy a Table from Another Database

(1) Open the database into which you want to copy a table.

(2) Point to Get External Data on the File menu, and then click Import.

(3) Double-click the database from which you want to import the table.

(4) Click the table or tables to import.

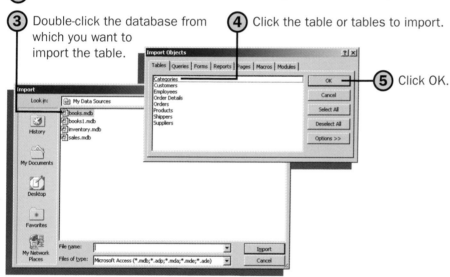

(5) Click OK.

> **TIP:** You can import data from other types of database objects by clicking the object type (such as Queries) in the Import Objects dialog box and then clicking the object from which you want to get your data.

> **TIP:** To deselect a table, click it again.

Relationships Explained

One-to-Many Relationships

One of the strengths of Access is the ability to create *relationships* between tables. As an example of a relationship, consider the Suppliers and Products tables from the Northwind sample database.

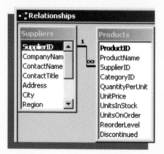

In the Northwind business case, every product comes from a single supplier—presumably the one with the best price. Of course, a supplier can sell more than one product, which means the Suppliers and Products tables are in a *one-to-many* relationship, with the Suppliers table on the "one" side and the Products table on the "many" side.

The Suppliers and Products tables may also be described as being in a *many-to-one* relationship, although you'll find thinking of their interaction as being in a one-to-many relationship to be much more useful.

Many-to-Many Relationships

It is also possible for two tables to be in a *many-to-many* relationship, in which multiple records from one table relate to multiple records from another table. As an example, consider the Products and Orders tables in the Northwind database: a product can be included in many orders and an order can include many products. The problem is that you can't relate the two tables directly without adding fields to

the Orders table to hold spots for more than one item, as in the following incorrect example.

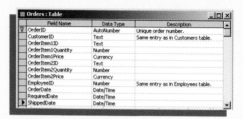

This table is poorly designed because it forces you to enter data about the customer and the order in each record instead of just once, and that an order can't be for more items than you have spots in the table. The proper way to manage the relationship is to create a *transition table*, which bridges the gap between the Products and Orders tables. In the Northwind database, the Order Details table is a transition table.

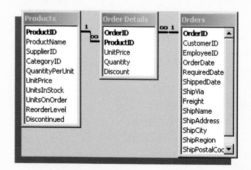

The Order Details table is on the "many" side of two one-to-many relationships—the first with the Products table and the second with the Orders table. By bridging the two tables, it lets you manage the relationship between the Orders and Products tables without resorting to improper table design.

Creating Relationships Between Tables

When the primary key from one table is present in another table, you can create a relationship between the two tables by dragging the primary key field to its corresponding field in the second table.

Define a Relationship

TIP: To delete a table from the Relationships window, right-click the table's title bar and then click Hide Table.

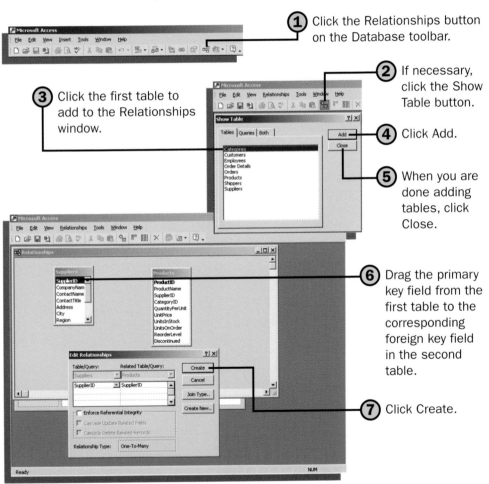

(1) Click the Relationships button on the Database toolbar.

(2) If necessary, click the Show Table button.

(3) Click the first table to add to the Relationships window.

(4) Click Add.

(5) When you are done adding tables, click Close.

TIP: The foreign key field and the primary key field don't have to have the same name...they just need to denote the same data.

(6) Drag the primary key field from the first table to the corresponding foreign key field in the second table.

(7) Click Create.

CAUTION: It is possible to add a table more than once—make sure you click the name of the table you want to add!

Enforcing Referential Integrity

When you create a relationship between two tables, you need to make sure that data in the two tables remains consistent. If you no longer order from a supplier, you would want all products from that supplier deleted from the Products table when you delete the supplier's data from the Suppliers table. Enforcing referential integrity lets you do that.

Enforce Referential Integrity

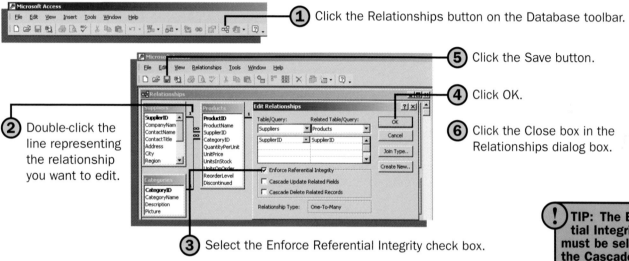

(1) Click the Relationships button on the Database toolbar.

(5) Click the Save button.

(4) Click OK.

(2) Double-click the line representing the relationship you want to edit.

(6) Click the Close box in the Relationships dialog box.

(3) Select the Enforce Referential Integrity check box.

- Selecting the Cascade Update Related Fields check box means Access will change the values in foreign key fields when the corresponding primary key field's value is changed.

- Selecting the Cascade Delete Related Records check box means that deleting a record from the primary field in a relationship will cause Access to delete all related records in the second table.

> **TIP: The Enforce Referential Integrity check box must be selected to make the Cascade Update Related Fields and Cascade Delete Related Records check boxes available.**

Customizing Fields

When you create a database table using a wizard, Microsoft Access assigns a data type and properties to each field in the table. When you create a table from scratch, or if you want to modify the settings Access applied to the table, you can change a field's properties so it stores data efficiently and interacts well with other fields in the database.

An important consideration of designing any database is ensuring that you and your colleagues enter table data accurately. Access gives you a number of tools to promote accurate data entry, such as requiring data entry in some fields and checking to make sure the value entered meets your expectations. You can also simplify data entry by assigning default values to fields or by providing templates to fill in when entering phone numbers and other common data patterns.

In this chapter, you'll learn how to:

● Add, delete, and arrange table fields.

● Change field data types and properties.

● Change field formats.

● Define input masks.

● Set default values.

Working with Tables

It's easy to create tables in Access, but you're not stuck with the first version of the table. After you've created a table, you can modify it by adding, deleting, and reordering fields.

Add a Field

① Click Tables on the Objects bar, click a table, and then click Design.

② Click the row selector of the row below where you want the new field to appear.

③ Click the Insert Rows button on the Table Design toolbar.

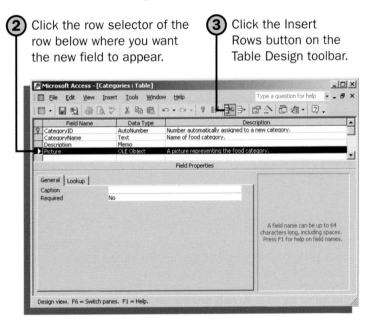

Delete a Field

① Click Tables on the Objects bar, click a table, and then click Design.

② Click the row selector of the row you want to delete.

③ Click the Delete Rows button on the Table Design toolbar.

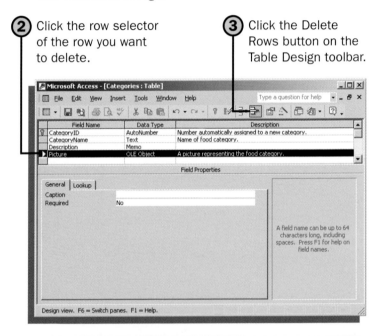

 CAUTION: Deleting a field gets rid of all the data in that field—it can't be retrieved. It's always a good idea to make a backup copy of a table when you make a significant change like deleting a field.

! **TIP:** If you add a field to a table after you have added data to it, remember to set aside time to fill in the new data for any existing records.

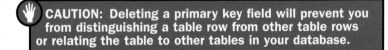 **CAUTION:** Deleting a primary key field will prevent you from distinguishing a table row from other table rows or relating the table to other tables in your database.

Arrange Fields

① Click Tables on the Objects bar, click a table, and then click Design.

③ Drag the row selector to the new position.

② Click the row selector of the row you want to move.

A line appears to show where the row will be moved in the table.

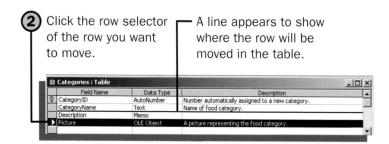

Assigning a Data Type

In Access, some operations such as arithmetic or date comparisons require you to assign the proper data type to a field. You have a number of data types to choose from, depending on your needs.

Pick a Data Type

① Open a table in Design view.

② Click in the Data Type box of the field you want to edit.

③ Click the down arrow.

④ Click the data type to assign to the field.

Available Data Types

Data Type	Description
Text	A series of numbers and letters of up to 255 characters
Memo	Same as the Text data type, with an upper limit of 65,536 characters
Number	Numeric data
Date/Time	Dates and times, between the years 100 and 9999
Currency	Primarily monetary amounts, but can also be used to specify the number of digits (with a maximum of 4) to the right of the decimal point
AutoNumber	A unique number for each row, either one greater than the value in the most recently created row or a random value
Yes/No	A Yes/No, On/Off, or True/False value
OLE Object	A file that is linked to or embedded within an Access table
Hyperlink	A link that opens a file, a location in a file, or a Web address
Lookup Wizard	A list of values derived from either an existing table (or query) field or from a list you enter directly

Viewing or Changing Field Properties

Every field has a number of properties, such as the maximum number of characters allowed in the field. The properties available to you are different for each data type.

View Field Properties

① Open a table in Design view.

② Click the row representing the field with the properties you want to change.

Build button

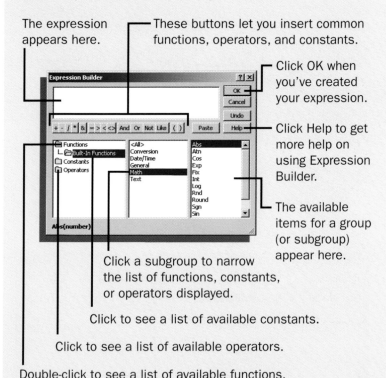

③ Click the name of the property you want to change.

④ Follow any of these steps:

- Type a new value for the property.

- Click the down arrow, and choose a new value from the list.

- Click the Build button to open the Expression Builder.

Introducing the Expression Builder

When you set a validation rule to check field data or when you create a calculation to find the total value of an order, you create an *expression* to evaluate the contents of one or more table fields. Rather than make you memorize how to identify the fields you want to use or which operators are available, you can use the controls in the Expression Builder to create your expressions quickly.

The expression appears here.

These buttons let you insert common functions, operators, and constants.

Click OK when you've created your expression.

Click Help to get more help on using Expression Builder.

The available items for a group (or subgroup) appear here.

Click a subgroup to narrow the list of functions, constants, or operators displayed.

Click to see a list of available constants.

Click to see a list of available operators.

Double-click to see a list of available functions.

Formatting Field Contents

Access lets you choose how to display the contents of data in your tables. For example, you can display the field's contents in all upper-case or lowercase letters, display characters in addition to the data entered into the field, or even change the color of the text. Adding formatting instructions only changes how data is displayed—it doesn't affect the data itself.

Change Field Format

① Open a table in Design view.

② Click the name of the field to format.

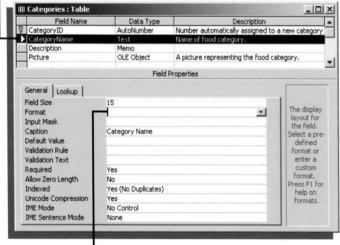

③ Type the formatting instructions in the Format property box.

> **!** **TIP: A down arrow will appear in the Format property box when the box is active; clicking the down arrow will display a list of recently used formats. To reuse a format, simply click it.**

Character	Resulting Format
!	Left align
<	Lowercase
>	Uppercase
"Text"	Display the text as it appears between the quotes. &" kg" displays the value "16" as "16 kg."
(space)	Insert a blank space.
\	Display the next character as entered. &\m displays the text "100" as "100m."
@	Require a character or space.
&	A character or space is optional.
*	Fill all blank spaces in the field with the named character. In a field with a maximum character property of eight, &*# displays "five" as "five####."
[color]	Display the field's contents in the named color.

Creating Input Masks

Databases are only as good as the data they hold, so it's important that you and your colleagues enter data correctly. You can guide data entry in text and date fields by creating an *input mask*, which gives you a template to follow when entering data in a field.

Define an Input Mask

① Open a table in Design view.

③ Click Input Mask.

② Click the field for which you want to create the input mask.

④ Click the Build button.

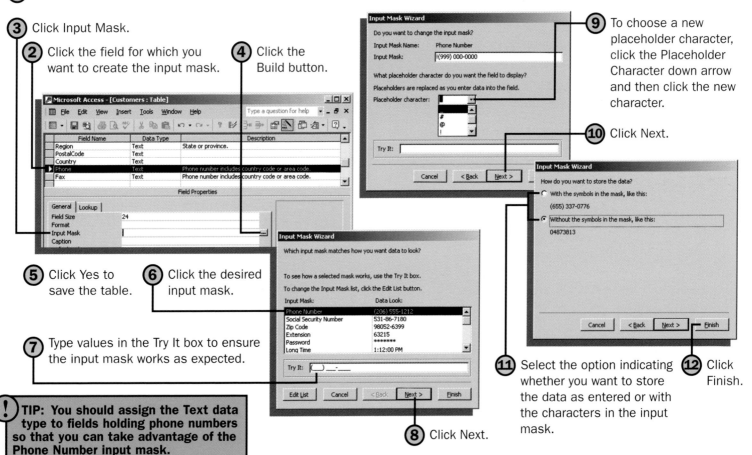

⑤ Click Yes to save the table.

⑥ Click the desired input mask.

⑦ Type values in the Try It box to ensure the input mask works as expected.

⑨ To choose a new placeholder character, click the Placeholder Character down arrow and then click the new character.

⑩ Click Next.

⑪ Select the option indicating whether you want to store the data as entered or with the characters in the input mask.

⑫ Click Finish.

⑧ Click Next.

> **! TIP:** If the data entered into a field is sensitive and shouldn't be read by someone watching as you or your colleague enter the data, choose the Password input mask.

> **! TIP:** You should assign the Text data type to fields holding phone numbers so that you can take advantage of the Phone Number input mask.

Editing an Input Mask

1 Click the field to which you assigned an input mask.

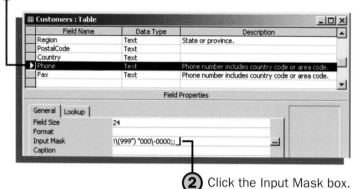

2 Click the Input Mask box.

3 Change the input mask using the available symbols.

Symbol	Description
0	Required digit (0 to 9)
9	Optional digit (0 to 9)
#	Any digit or space
L	Required letter (A to Z)
?	Optional letter (A to Z)
>	Makes following characters uppercase
<	Makes following characters lowercase
A	Required alphanumeric character
a	Optional alphanumeric character
&	Required character or space
C	Optional character or space

! **TIP: You can also reopen the Input Mask wizard by clicking the Build button at the right edge of the Input Mask property box.**

Assigning Required Fields and Requiring Data Entry

Some data is more important than other data. For example, a salesperson might need to know a contact's phone number but not necessarily the contact's address. You can tell Access to prevent someone from moving beyond a required field without entering a value. For text and memo fields, you can require users to enter at least one character of text.

Require Data Entry

1 Open a table in Design view.

2 Click the field for which you want to require data entry.

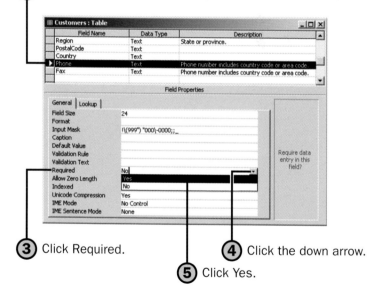

3 Click Required.

4 Click the down arrow.

5 Click Yes.

Disallow Zero-Length Strings

1 Open a table in Design view.

2 Click the text or memo field for which you want to require the user to enter at least one character of text.

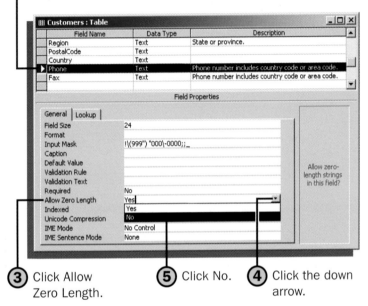

3 Click Allow Zero Length.

5 Click No.

4 Click the down arrow.

Setting Default Values

When you enter data, you'll often find that you enter the same value in a field many times. For example, most of your customers might come from the United States, but you have a Country field for those customers outside the United States. Setting a default value for a field saves you the trouble of entering the expected data over and over while still allowing you to edit the value if needed.

Assign a Default Value

1 Open a table in Design view.

2 Click the field to which you want to assign the default value.

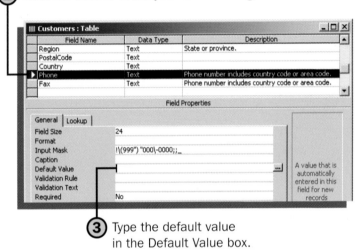

3 Type the default value in the Default Value box.

> **!** **TIP:** As your needs change, you should periodically review any default values you've set to be sure you aren't slowing yourself down by deleting incorrect data.

Indexing Field Values

When you create an index of a field's values, Access maintains an internal record of the values in a field, which the program can then use to find table records with specific values. Access always keeps an index of a table's primary key field's values.

Create an Index

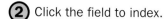 Open a table in Design view.

② Click the field to index.

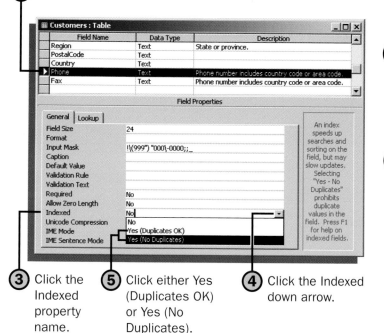

③ Click the Indexed property name.

⑤ Click either Yes (Duplicates OK) or Yes (No Duplicates).

④ Click the Indexed down arrow.

CAUTION: Access updates all of its indexes every time you add or update a table record. Creating unneeded indexes can greatly slow down data entry, especially on older systems.

TIP: Indexes work best in fields with lots of different values. In large tables, indexing the values in commonly used fields lets Access find what you're looking for quickly.

TRY THIS! Open the Northwind sample database, click Tables on the Objects bar, click Products, and then click Design. Click any cell in the ProductName row of the design grid, and then click Indexed in the Field Properties section of the dialog box. Click the down arrow that appears, and then click Yes (No Duplicates). This change requires every new product entered into the table to have a unique name. This specific change works for Northwind, which carries unique products, but may not work for a business that buys common items from more than one supplier.

Validating Data Entry

Some categories of data, such as credit limits or the date someone joined a club, must meet certain criteria. You can make sure data entered into field meets those criteria (for example, all credit limits are $5000 or less) by performing *data validation*. When a user tries to enter data that isn't appropriate for the field, you can display a message letting him or her know what went wrong.

Perform Data Validation

1 Open a table in Design view.

2 Click Validation Rule.

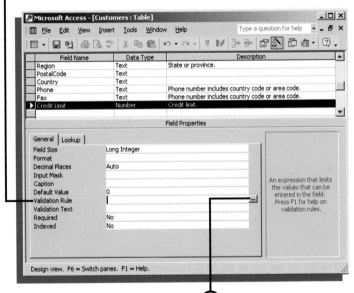

3 Click the Build button.

4 Create the validation rule in the Expression Builder.

5 Click OK.

Set Validation Text

1 Open a table in Design view.

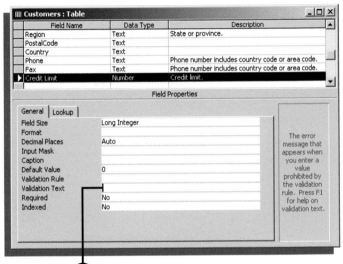

2 Type your validation text in the Validation Text box.

! **TIP: You can type your validation rule, such as <=5000, directly into the Validation Rule box.**

Creating a Lookup Field

Many times the data you need to enter in one table can be found in another table. In the Northwind database, for example, if you add a new product, you must assign it to a category. Rather than make you open the Categories table separately and find the value you need, Access lets you display those values in a list. You can also create your own list, rather than draw values from an existing source.

Define a Field as a Lookup Field

① Open a table in Design view, click the field to define as a lookup field, click the Data Type cell, click the down arrow, and then click Lookup Wizard.

② Select the I Want The Lookup Column To Look Up The Values In A Table Or Query option.

③ Click Next.

④ Click the table or query to provide the values, and then click Next.

⑤ Click the first field to provide the values.

⑥ Click Add.

⑦ Repeat steps 5 and 6 to add more fields.

⑧ Click Next.

⑨ Click Finish.

> **TIP:** You should leave the Hide key column check box selected so the person using the lookup column will only see the values in the field you want them to see, not the values in the primary key field.

> **TIP:** You should strongly consider using lookup fields where spelling errors of even a single letter could throw off your data.

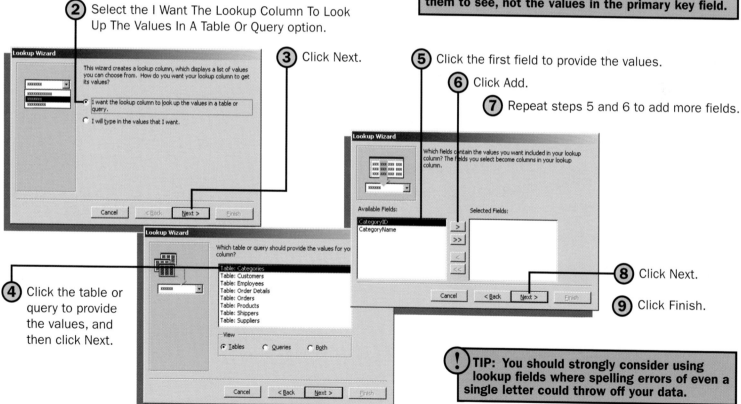

Draw Lookup Values from a Data List

(1) Open a table in Design view, click the field to
define as a lookup field, click the Data Type cell,
click the down arrow, and click the Lookup Wizard.

(2) Select the I
Will Type In
The Values
That I Want
option.

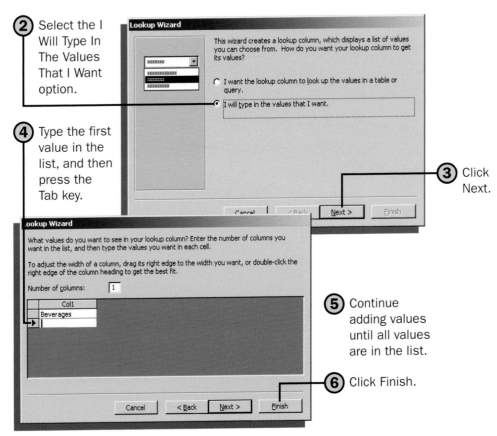

(4) Type the first
value in the
list, and then
press the
Tab key.

(3) Click
Next.

(5) Continue
adding values
until all values
are in the list.

(6) Click Finish.

6

Customizing Tables

In Chapter 5, you saw how to change a table's structure by working with the table in Design view. This chapter shows you how to work with a table in Datasheet view, where the table data is displayed in a datasheet in which each column represents a table field and each row represents a table record. Changing how your data is displayed in Datasheet view can make your table easier to read and work with—for example, you might change the order of fields in a table to reflect the natural order you and your colleagues follow when entering data from a paper form into the table.

In this chapter, you'll learn how to:

● Find and replace text.

● Streamline data entry.

● Move and modify table columns and rows.

● Work with subdatasheets.

● Filter table records.

Finding and Replacing Text

After you've entered data into a table, you might need to search the table for a particular word or, if one of your suppliers changes the name of a product, replace some or all instances of a word or phrase. You can do just that using the Find and Replace tools in Microsoft Access.

Find Text

1 Click Tables on the Objects bar.

3 Click Open.

8 Click Find Next.

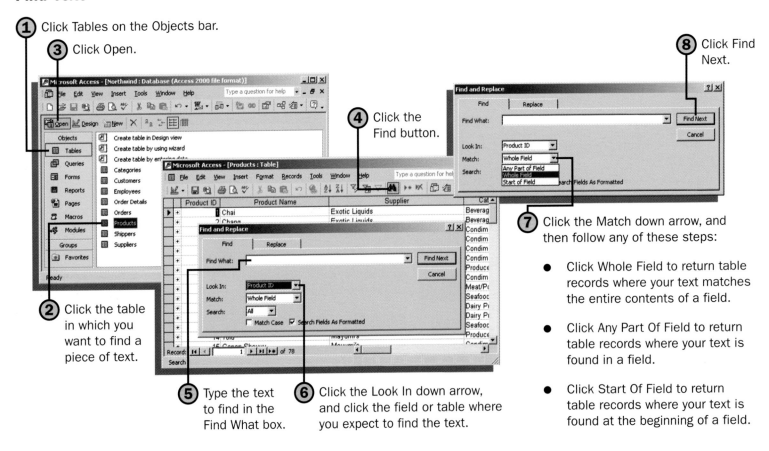

4 Click the Find button.

2 Click the table in which you want to find a piece of text.

5 Type the text to find in the Find What box.

6 Click the Look In down arrow, and click the field or table where you expect to find the text.

7 Click the Match down arrow, and then follow any of these steps:

- Click Whole Field to return table records where your text matches the entire contents of a field.

- Click Any Part Of Field to return table records where your text is found in a field.

- Click Start Of Field to return table records where your text is found at the beginning of a field.

Replace Text

1 Click Tables on the Objects bar.

3 Click Open. **2** Click the table in which you want to find a piece of text.

5 Click Replace.

4 Click the Find button.

10 Click Find Next to locate the first instance of the text to be replaced.

11 Click Replace.

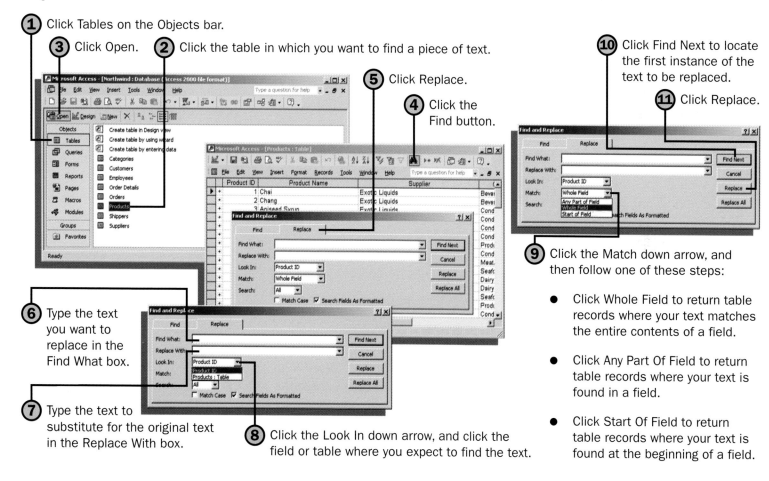

6 Type the text you want to replace in the Find What box.

7 Type the text to substitute for the original text in the Replace With box.

8 Click the Look In down arrow, and click the field or table where you expect to find the text.

9 Click the Match down arrow, and then follow one of these steps:

- Click Whole Field to return table records where your text matches the entire contents of a field.

- Click Any Part Of Field to return table records where your text is found in a field.

- Click Start Of Field to return table records where your text is found at the beginning of a field.

Entering Data Using AutoCorrect

When you enter data into a table, Access examines what you've typed and corrects any common spelling errors it knows about. You can also add your own AutoCorrect values to streamline data entry—for example, you could have Access recognize the abbreviation "sarsp" and replace it with "sarsaparilla."

Add Text with AutoCorrect

1 Click Tables on the Objects bar.

3 Click Open. **2** Click the table in which you want to find a piece of text.

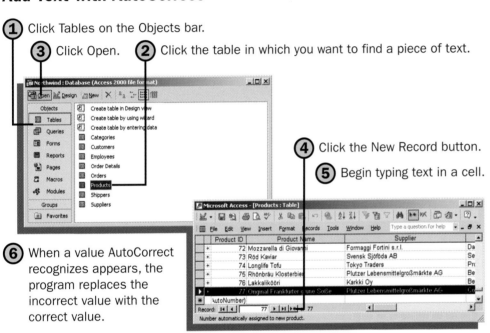

4 Click the New Record button.

5 Begin typing text in a cell.

6 When a value AutoCorrect recognizes appears, the program replaces the incorrect value with the correct value.

Turn AutoCorrect On or Off

1 Choose AutoCorrect Options from the Tools menu.

2 Do either of the following:

- Select the Replace Text As You Type check box to turn on AutoCorrect.

- Clear the Replace Text As You Type check box to turn off AutoCorrect.

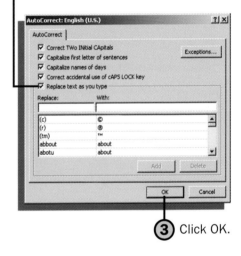

3 Click OK.

Add AutoCorrect Values

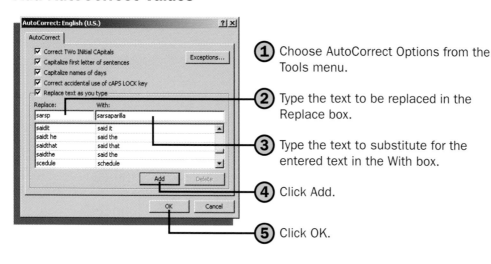

(1) Choose AutoCorrect Options from the Tools menu.

(2) Type the text to be replaced in the Replace box.

(3) Type the text to substitute for the entered text in the With box.

(4) Click Add.

(5) Click OK.

TRY THIS: Choose the AutoCorrect Options command from the Tools menu. Then, type bev **in the Replace box, type** beverage **in the With box, and click Add. Click OK to close the AutoCorrect dialog box. Now every time you type** bev**, AutoCorrect will replace it with "beverage."**

Adding and Editing Text

Once you open a table, you can edit the existing data, add new data, or copy data from one cell and paste it into another. The Office Clipboard, which is new in Access 2002, keeps track of the last 24 items you've cut or copied. If you want Access to undo the last change you made, you can do so by clicking the Undo button.

Select Text

● Move the mouse pointer over a cell until the pointer turns into a white cross, and then click the cell.

● Double-click a word to select it.

● Drag the mouse pointer over text to select it.

Products : Table		
Product ID	Product Name	
1 Chai		Exotic Liquids
2 Chang		Exotic Liquids
3 Aniseed Syrup		Exotic Liquids

Delete Text

● Click to the right of the text to be deleted, and press Backspace to delete it one character at a time.

● Select the text, and press Delete.

4	Chef Anton's Cajun Seasoning
5	Chef Anton's Gumbo Mix
6	Grandma's Boysenberry Spread
7	Uncle Bob's Organic Dried Pears
8	Northwoods Cranberry Sauce
9	Mishi Kobe Niku

Copy and Paste Text

① Select the text you want to copy.

② Click the Copy button.

④ Click the Paste button.

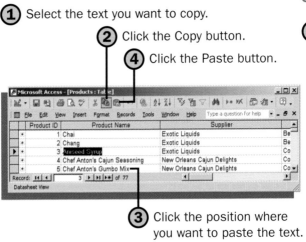

③ Click the position where you want to paste the text.

Copy and Paste Items Using the Office Clipboard
⊕ NEW FEATURE

① If necessary, choose Office Clipboard from the Edit menu.

② Select the contents of a cell, and click Copy.

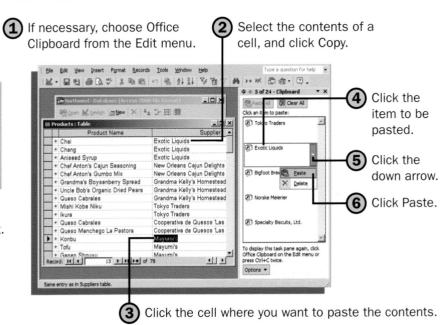

④ Click the item to be pasted.

⑤ Click the down arrow.

⑥ Click Paste.

③ Click the cell where you want to paste the contents.

Undoing Operations ⊕ NEW FEATURE

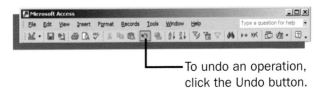

To undo an operation, click the Undo button.

Manipulating Columns

You can change how data is displayed in your datasheet by changing the order of the table's columns. You can also add or delete fields by inserting a column (which creates a new field) or deleting a column (which deletes the field it represented). If you want to copy the contents of a column to another table, or even to another Office document, you can do so easily.

Relocate a Column

2 Drag the column to its new position in the datasheet. A vertical black line appears on the edge between the two columns where the moved column will be pasted.

1 Click the column head of the column you want to move.

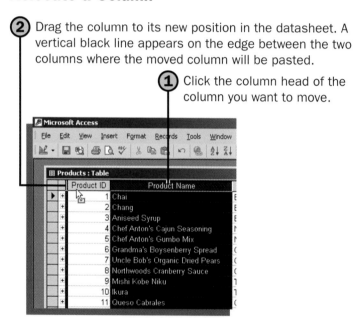

Insert a Column

1 Right-click the column head of the column to the right of where you want the new column to appear.

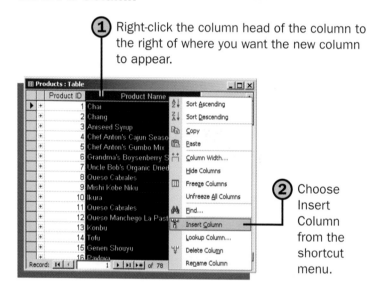

2 Choose Insert Column from the shortcut menu.

 CAUTION: Be sure to release the mouse button after you click the column head; if you don't, you'll select more than one column instead of moving the column you want to move.

Rename a Column

1 Right-click the column head of the column you want to rename.

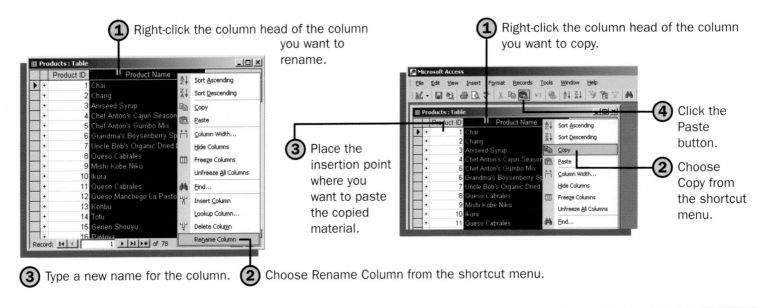

3 Type a new name for the column.   **2** Choose Rename Column from the shortcut menu.

Copy a Column

1 Right-click the column head of the column you want to copy.

3 Place the insertion point where you want to paste the copied material.

4 Click the Paste button.

2 Choose Copy from the shortcut menu.

Modifying Columns and Rows

The standard height of datasheet rows is just enough to display the contents of a row. While that setting fits a lot of data on a sheet, it doesn't always make it easy to read. You can increase the height of the rows in your worksheet to add some padding; similarly, you can change a column's width to show more or less of its contents.

Change Row Height

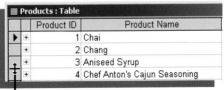

2 Drag the edge up or down.

1 Move the mouse pointer over an edge of the row selector of the row you want to resize.

> **!** **TIP:** To change the width of more than one column, select the columns to change, move the mouse pointer over any of the columns' edges, and drag to the desired width. Every selected column will take on the new setting. You can't change just one row's height, though; any change you make will be applied to every row.

Change Column Width

① Move the mouse pointer over an edge of the column selector of the column you want to resize.

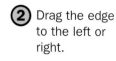 Drag the edge to the left or right.

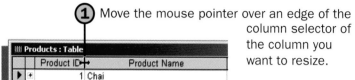

Viewing a Subdatasheet

When two tables are in a one-to-many relationship, you can create a *subdatasheet* that displays records from the table on the "many" side of the relationship. A plus sign will appear next to the key field of the datasheet on the "one" side of the relationship, indicating a subdatasheet is available.

Open and Close a Subdatasheet

① Open a table. **②** Click the plus sign next to the value for which you want to see records in the related subdatasheet.

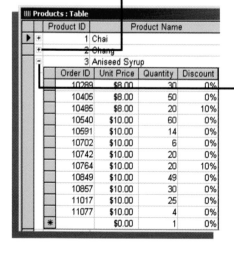

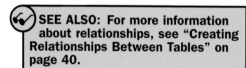 Click the minus sign to hide the subdatasheet.

> **SEE ALSO: For more information about relationships, see "Creating Relationships Between Tables" on page 40.**

Create a Subdatasheet

1 Open a table.

2 Choose Subdatasheet from the Insert menu.

8 Click OK.

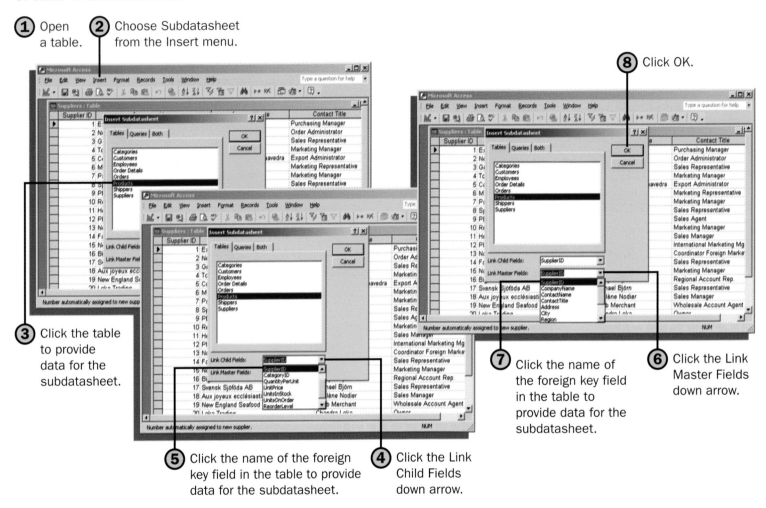

3 Click the table to provide data for the subdatasheet.

7 Click the name of the foreign key field in the table to provide data for the subdatasheet.

6 Click the Link Master Fields down arrow.

5 Click the name of the foreign key field in the table to provide data for the subdatasheet.

4 Click the Link Child Fields down arrow.

Filtering Table Records

Often you will be interested in only part of the records in a table. For example, you might want to find all of your customers or suppliers from a particular state or country. You can narrow the records shown in a table by creating a filter, which hides records not meeting your criteria. The records aren't erased, though; when you remove the filter, they're displayed normally.

Filter Table Records

1 Click Tables on the Objects bar.

3 Click Open.

5 Click the Filter By Selection button.

4 Select the text to serve as the base for the filter.

2 Click the table you want to work with.

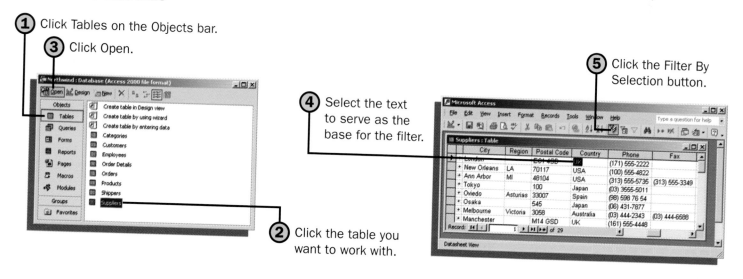

Filter by Form

1 Click Tables on the Objects bar.

3 Click Open.

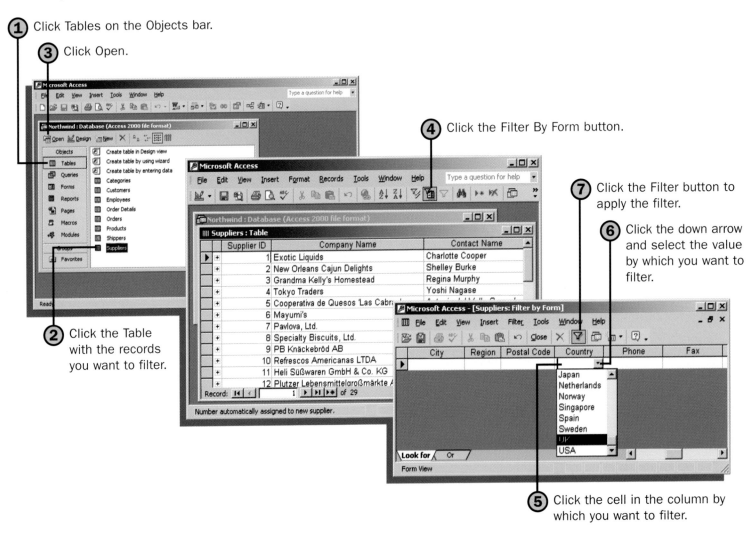

4 Click the Filter By Form button.

7 Click the Filter button to apply the filter.

6 Click the down arrow and select the value by which you want to filter.

2 Click the Table with the records you want to filter.

5 Click the cell in the column by which you want to filter.

Filter Records by the Contents of More than One Column

① Open a table in Datasheet view.

② Point to Filter on the Records menu, and then click Advanced Filter/Sort.

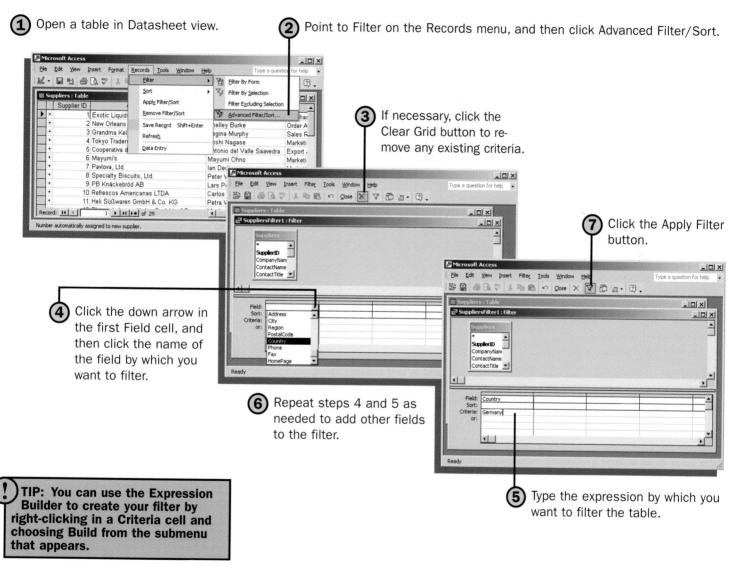

③ If necessary, click the Clear Grid button to remove any existing criteria.

⑦ Click the Apply Filter button.

④ Click the down arrow in the first Field cell, and then click the name of the field by which you want to filter.

⑥ Repeat steps 4 and 5 as needed to add other fields to the filter.

⑤ Type the expression by which you want to filter the table.

! TIP: You can use the Expression Builder to create your filter by right-clicking in a Criteria cell and choosing Build from the submenu that appears.

Remove a Filter

1 Choose the Remove Filter/Sort command from the Records menu.

Filter by Selection

1 Open a table in Datasheet view.

2 Select the value by which you want to filter the table.

3 Point to Filter on the Records menu, and then click Filter By Selection.

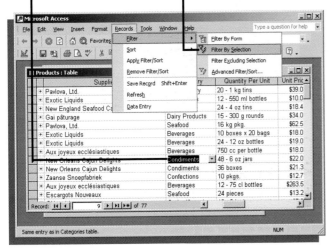

Filter Excluding Selection

1 Open a table in Datasheet view.

2 Select the value you want to exclude from the table.

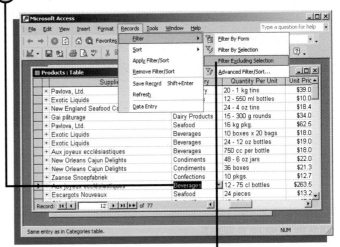

3 Point to Filter on the Records menu, and then click Filter Excluding Selection.

TRY THIS: Open the Northwind sample database, and then open the Products table in Datasheet view. Click the Filter By Form button. Click any cell in the Category column, and then click the down arrow that appears in the selected cell. Choose Beverages from the list that appears. Click the Filter button once to apply the filter and again to remove the filter.

7 Creating Forms

One of the nice things about Microsoft Access 2002 is that it makes it easy for you to view existing table data and even add new data using forms. A *form* is a database object that lets you enter and view table data without viewing the table in datasheet mode. Instead, you can create a form that spaces the data out on the page, limit the number of table fields displayed so that only the most important or relevant data is shown, and modify the form once you've created it to make the form easier to use.

In this chapter, you'll learn how to:

● Create a form with the Form Wizard.

● Modify an existing form.

● Add, remove, and edit form controls.

● Create a subform.

Creating a Form with the Form Wizard

Access makes it easy for you to create forms based on the tables in your database. By using the Form Wizard, you can choose the data source, the type of the form, and the form's appearance.

Step Through the Form Wizard

1 Click Forms on the Objects bar.

2 Double-click Create Form By Using Wizard.

3 Click the Tables/Queries down arrow.

4 Click the table to provide the values and structure for the form.

5 Click a field in the Available Fields box, and then click either of the following:

- Add to add the selected field.
- Add All to add all fields to the form.

6 Click Next.

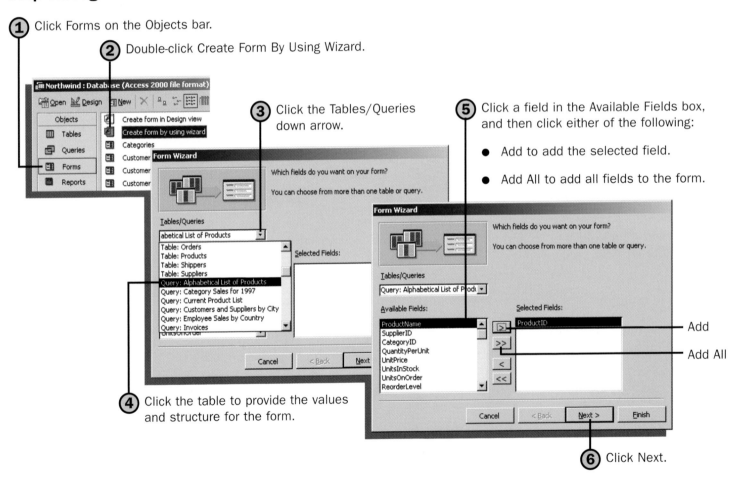

⑦ Select the layout for the form.

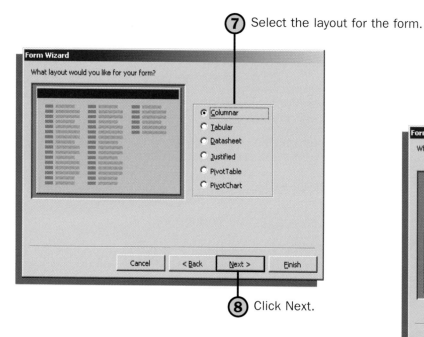

⑧ Click Next.

⑨ Click the name of the style for the form.

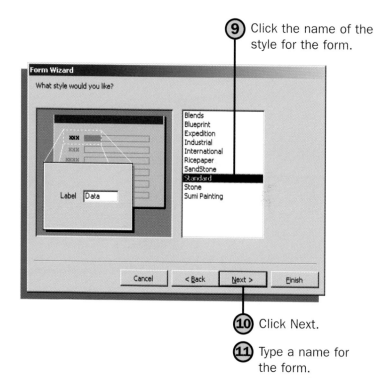

⑩ Click Next.

⑪ Type a name for the form.

⑫ Click Finish.

! TIP: You can remove a field from the Selected Fields box by clicking the field and then clicking Remove. Clicking Remove All clears the Selected Fields box.

! TIP: You should create a sample form of each of the four main types (Columnar, Tabular, Justified, and Datasheet) to see which type will best meet your needs in a particular situation.

Creating a Form in Design View

If you'd rather not use the Form Wizard to create a form, you can open a blank form and add controls by hand.

Create a New Form from Scratch

(1) Click Forms on the Objects bar.

(2) Double-click Create Form In Design View.

(4) Click Data.

(3) Click the Properties button.

(7) Click the Close box.

(8) Drag a field from the Field List box to the form.

(5) Click the Record Source down arrow.

(6) Click the table to provide the structure for the form.

(9) Click the Close box to hide the Field List box.

(10) Click the Save button.

(11) Type a name for the form.

(12) Click OK.

TRY THIS: Open the Northwind sample database, click Forms on the Objects Bar, and then double-click Create A New Form In Design View. After the form appears, click the Properties toolbar button and then, if necessary, click the Data tab. Click the Data Source property name, click the down arrow that appears, and then click Products. Click the Close box to close the Properties box, and then click the Save button. Type ProductSample in the dialog box, and click OK. You have just identified the Products table as the data source for the form. Now when you open the Field List box, the fields from the Products table will be available for use on the form.

Modifying an Existing Form

Just as you can create a form from scratch, you can open a form in Design View to add and delete controls, change a form's appearance, or add and delete fields.

Open a Form for Editing

(3) Click Design to open the form in Design view.

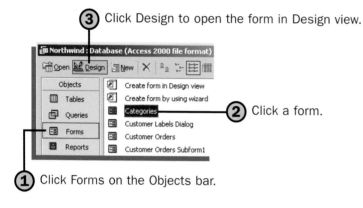

(2) Click a form.

(1) Click Forms on the Objects bar.

Add a Field to a Form

● Drag the field from the Field List box to the desired spot on the form.

Field

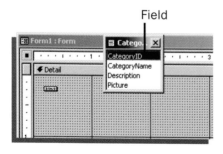

Display or Hide the Field List

● Click the Field List button to display the Field List box.

● Click the Close box to hide the Field List box.

Field List box

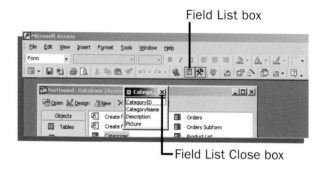

Field List Close box

> **SEE ALSO:** For more information about modifying forms, see Chapter 10, "Beautifying Forms and Reports."

> **TIP:** When you have a form open in Design view, you can also display the Field List box by pressing F8.

Adding and Deleting Form Controls

After you open a form in Design view, you can add or remove text boxes, option buttons, and images from the form. You can also modify a control's properties to change the control's appearance or to define where the control gets its data.

Add a Control with a Wizard

① Open a form in Design view. **②** If necessary, click the Toolbox button.

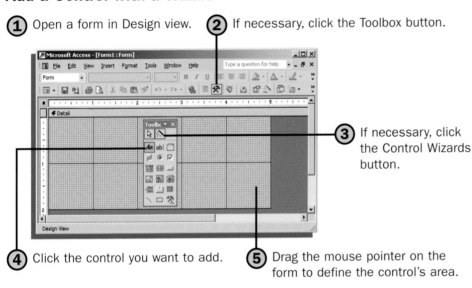

③ If necessary, click the Control Wizards button.

④ Click the control you want to add. **⑤** Drag the mouse pointer on the form to define the control's area.

⑥ Follow the steps in the wizard to define the contents of the control.

SEE ALSO: For information about setting a control's properties if the control doesn't have an associated wizard, see "Modify Control Properties" on the next page.

Delete a Control

① Right-click the control.

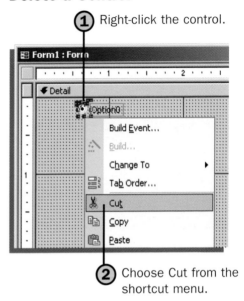

② Choose Cut from the shortcut menu.

CAUTION: Be sure to click the control itself, not the label next to the control.

TIP: You can set or change a control's data source by opening the control's Properties box, clicking the Data tab, and setting the Control Source property.

Modify Control Properties

① Click the control.   ② Click the Properties button.   ③ Click the property to change.   Build button

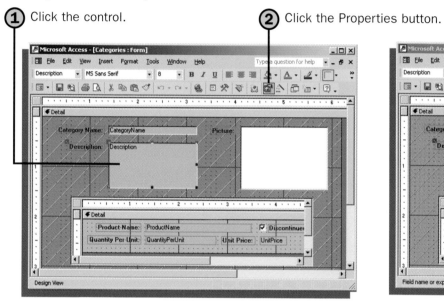

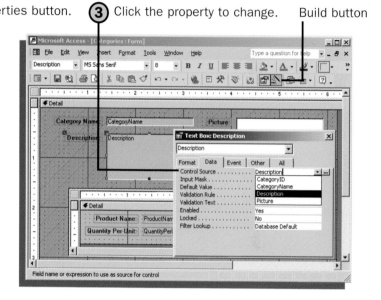

④ Follow any of these steps:

- ● Type a new value in the text box next to the property name.

- ● Click the down arrow, and select a new property from the list that appears.

- ● Click the Build button, and use the dialog box that appears to select or construct a new value.

Available Control Types

Control	Description
Label	Text that is not tied to a field or other control.
Text Box	A control that holds the contents of an existing table or query field or that has been typed in by a user.
Toggle Button	A button that can either be off or on, representing an independent value of off/on, true/false, or yes/no.
Option Button	An independent option that represents an independent value. When grouped, only one option button may be selected at a time.
Check Box	An independent option that can be selected or cleared. When grouped, more than one check box may be selected.
List Box	A control that allows a user to pick a value from a list entered by the form's creator or that is derived from a table or query.
Combo Box	A control that allows a user to enter a value or pick a value from a list entered by the form's creator or that is derived from a table or query.
Command Button	A button that, when clicked, executes a macro or other set of instructions linked to the button.
Image	A control that holds an image or graphic.
Unbound Object Frame	A control that holds a linked file.
Bound Object Frame	A control that holds an embedded file.
Page Break	A control that separates a form into two (or more) printed pages.
Tab Page	A control with multiple pages, accessed by folder tabs at the top of the control.
Subform/Subreport	A form or report that displays records from a form or report on the "many" side of a one-to-many relationship.
Line	A control that lets you draw a line on a form.
Rectangle	A control that lets you draw a rectangle.
Option Group	An outline you place around a group of controls such as check boxes or option buttons. Only one control in the group may be selected at a time.
More Controls	A control that, when selected, displays a new window containing more controls you can add to your form.

Creating a Subform

When you create a form that shows the records from a table on the "one" side of a one-to-many relationship, you can create a subform to display records from the table on the "many" side of the relationship.

Add a Subform

② Click Design.

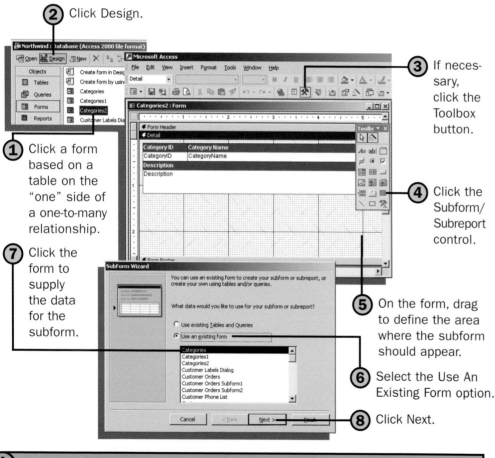

① Click a form based on a table on the "one" side of a one-to-many relationship.

③ If necessary, click the Toolbox button.

④ Click the Subform/Subreport control.

⑦ Click the form to supply the data for the subform.

⑤ On the form, drag to define the area where the subform should appear.

⑥ Select the Use An Existing Form option.

⑧ Click Next.

SEE ALSO: For more information about relationships, see "Creating Relationships Between Tables" on page 40.

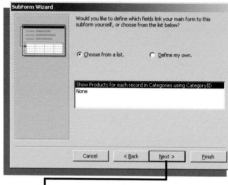

⑨ Click Next to have the wizard draw the values from the form you selected.

⑩ Type **Subform** after the end of the form name.

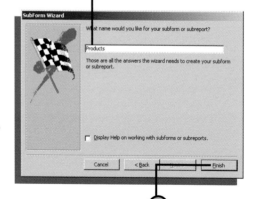

⑪ Click Finish.

! TIP: You can get help on using subforms and subreports by selecting the Display Help On Working With Subforms Or Subreports check box and clicking Finish.

Changing Subform Views

When you add a subform to a form, Access usually displays the subform in Form view. If you'd rather have the subform presented in another view, such as Datasheet view, you can change the view by right-clicking the subform and choosing the desired view from the shortcut menu. You can also have Access display the subform in Datasheet view (or any other view) by default—all you need to do is set the subform's properties so that Access knows what you want.

Display a Subform in Datasheet View

① Click Forms on the Objects bar.

② Click the form containing the subform.

③ Click Open.

> **TIP:** When you create a subform based on an existing table or query, Access looks for an existing form based on that table or query. If it finds one, it uses that form as the subform.

④ Right-click the subform, point to Subform on the shortcut menu, and then click Datasheet.

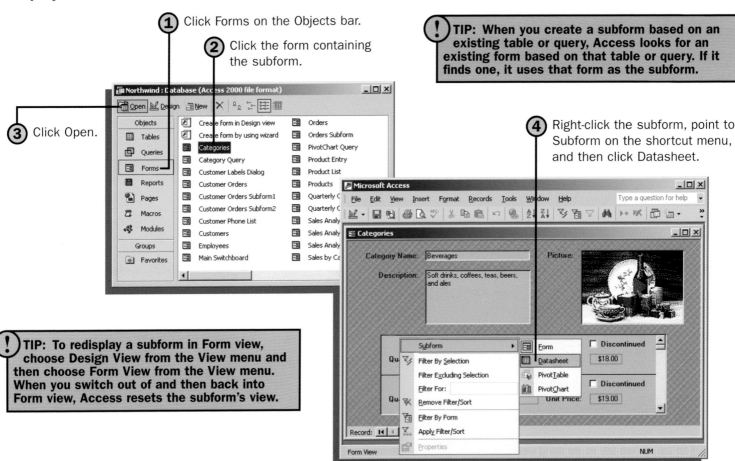

> **TIP:** To redisplay a subform in Form view, choose Design View from the View menu and then choose Form View from the View menu. When you switch out of and then back into Form view, Access resets the subform's view.

Change the Default View of a Subform

(1) Click Forms on the Objects bar.

(2) Click the form containing the subform.

(3) Click Design.

(5) If necessary, click the Format tab.

(6) Click Default View.

(7) Click the Default View down arrow.

(8) Click Datasheet.

(9) Click the Close box.

(10) Click the Save button on the Standard toolbar to save your changes.

(4) Double-click the Form Selector on the subform to display the subform's Properties box.

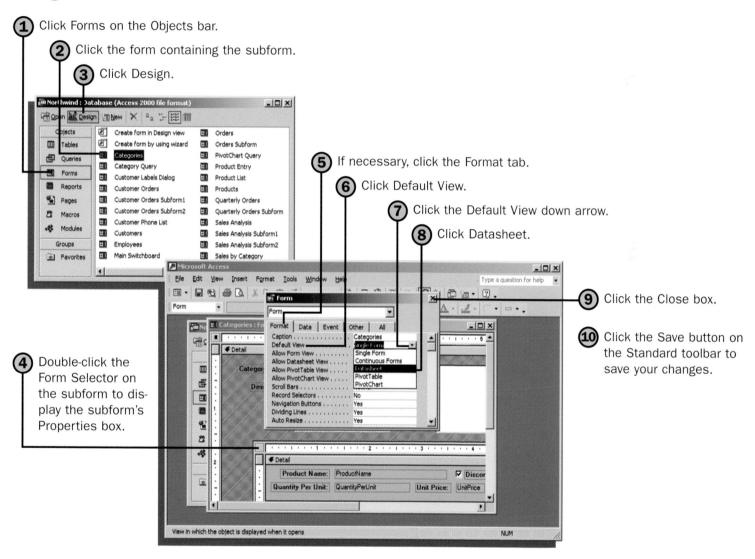

Creating Queries

The database object used to store data is the *table*, but even the best-designed table has limitations. For example, if a table holds more than a few dozen records, it's difficult to look through the table and find records that meet a particular criterion. You may want to display all orders from a specific customer without having to wade through the entire table to find them.

Enter the *query*. A query is an Access object that lets you find just those table records you're interested in, whether you want to see all orders from customers in Germany or to identify customers who have never placed an order. You can also create queries that let you and your colleagues type in the value for which they want to search; rather than always search for orders by customers in Germany, you could create a query that asks which country to look for.

In this chapter, you'll learn how to:

● Create a select query.

● Modify an existing query.

● Focus query results.

● Calculate values in queries.

● Write query results to a new table.

● Use a query to update table values.

Introducing Query Types

When you want to retrieve table records that meet particular criteria, you create a query. The type of query you create, however, depends on the records you want to return and what, if anything, you want Access to do with the results.

The most basic query type is the *select query*, which reaches into one or more database tables and locates records. While you can have Access return every record in a table, you can also choose which fields will be displayed in the results. For example, you could get information about customers that placed an order in a given month and, instead of displaying every field relating to the company, just display the company's name. You can also limit the records returned by the query by specifying one or more *criteria*, or rules the query uses when deciding which table rows to return.

A version of the select query is the *parameter query*. Like a select query, the parameter query uses one or more criteria to limit the records returned by the query. The difference, however, is that a parameter query lets the person running the query specify the criterion Access will use to decide whether or not to return a specific record. You can add a message to the criteria entry dialog box that lets the searcher know what kind of value to enter.

A separate type of query is the *action query*, which makes changes to the physical make-up of your database. You'll see two types of action queries in this chapter: the *update query*, which lets you change values in a table; and the *make-table query*, which writes query results to a new table in the current database (or another database entirely).

The final query type discussed in this chapter is the *crosstab query*. Unlike a select query, which presents its results in a datasheet, a crosstab query presents its results in a layout like that of a spreadsheet, as shown in the following graphic.

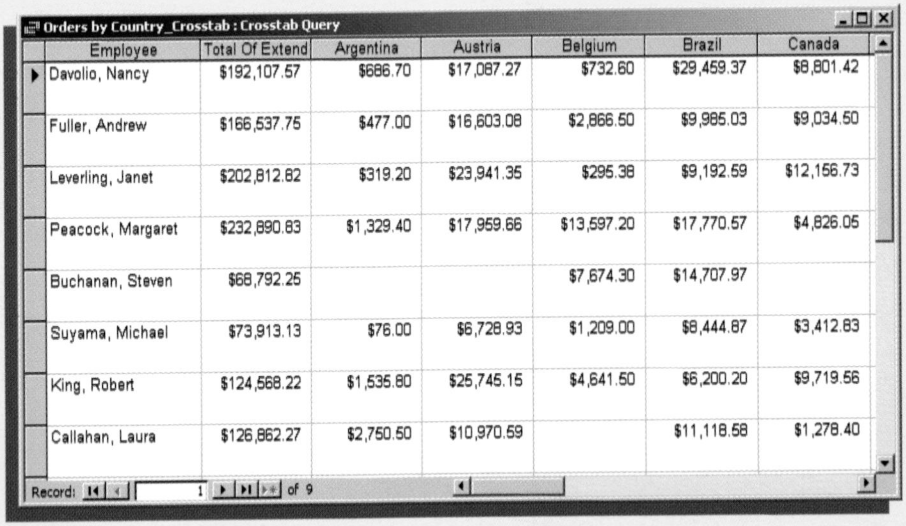

Orders by Country_Crosstab : Crosstab Query

Employee	Total Of Extend	Argentina	Austria	Belgium	Brazil	Canada
Davolio, Nancy	$192,107.57	$686.70	$17,087.27	$732.60	$29,459.37	$8,801.42
Fuller, Andrew	$166,537.75	$477.00	$16,603.08	$2,866.50	$9,985.03	$9,034.50
Leverling, Janet	$202,812.82	$319.20	$23,941.35	$295.38	$9,192.59	$12,156.73
Peacock, Margaret	$232,890.83	$1,329.40	$17,959.66	$13,597.20	$17,770.57	$4,826.05
Buchanan, Steven	$68,792.25			$7,674.30	$14,707.97	
Suyama, Michael	$73,913.13	$76.00	$6,728.93	$1,209.00	$8,444.87	$3,412.83
King, Robert	$124,568.22	$1,535.80	$25,745.15	$4,641.50	$6,200.20	$9,719.56
Callahan, Laura	$126,862.27	$2,750.50	$10,970.59		$11,118.58	$1,278.40

Record: 1 of 9

Every value in the body of the query's results is related to two other values. In this case, the values are the country from which orders were placed and the EmployeeID of the employee who made the sale.

As in a spreadsheet, you can choose the mathematical operation Access uses to summarize the data in the body of the crosstab query's results. Available operations include finding a sum, an average, the number of occurrences (as in the crosstab query results shown on the opposite page), or even the minimum or maximum value.

Once you've created a query, you can run it by double-clicking the query's icon in the Database window. If you have the query open in Design view, you can run the query by clicking the Run button.

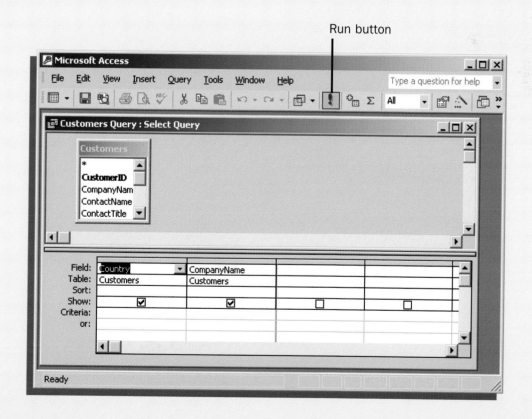

Run button

Creating a Query Using the Query Wizard

When you create a basic select query, you identify the table (or tables) with the data you want to find, name the fields to appear in the query results, and then save the query. The Query Wizard walks you through the process, making it easy to identify the tables and fields to appear in your query.

Step Through the Query Wizard

① Click Queries on the Objects bar.

② Double-click Create Query By Using Wizard.

③ Click the Tables/Queries down arrow.

④ Click the table or query with the fields you want to use in your query.

⑤ Click the field to include in the query's results.

⑥ Click Add.

⑦ Repeat steps 5–6 to add more fields (and steps 3–4 to change the table or query from which you draw fields).

⑧ Click Next.

⑨ Type a name for your query.

⑩ Click Finish.

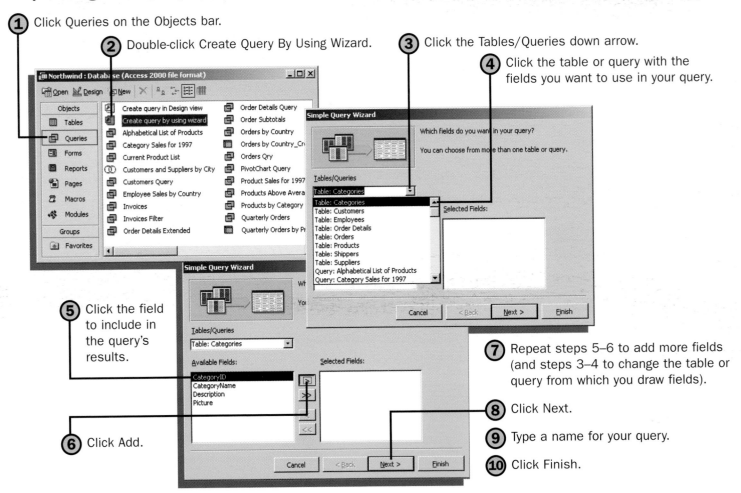

Editing a Query in Design View

After you create a query, you can modify it by opening it in Design view. In Design view, you can add a table to the Query design area, add or remove query fields, or even add every field from a table with one fell swoop.

Open a Query for Editing

1. Click Queries on the Objects bar.

2. Click a query.

3. Click Design to open the query in Design view.

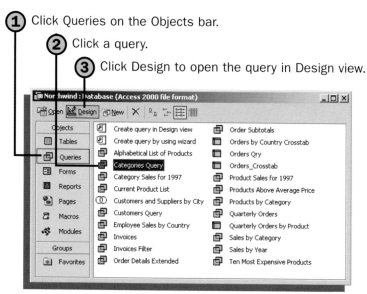

Add a Table to a Query

1. Open the query in Design view.

3. Click the table to add.

2. Click the Show Tables button.

4. Click Add.

5. Click Close.

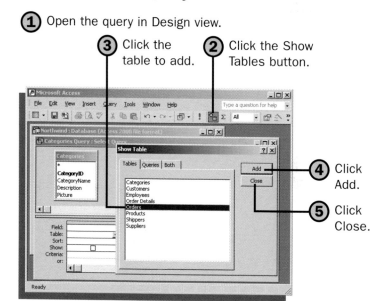

Add a Field to a Query

① Open the query in Design view.

② Drag a field to a Field cell.

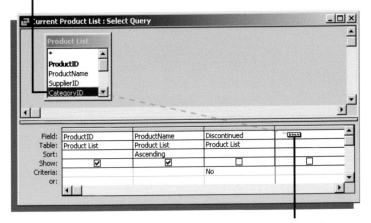

Target Field cell

! **TIP:** To add every field from a table to a query's results, drag the asterisk from the table's box in the table area to a Field cell in the query design grid.

! **TIP:** For a query with more than one table to return meaningful results, the two tables must be linked by a relationship.

Create a Query in Design View

① Click Queries on the Objects bar.

② Double-click Create Query In Design View.

③ Add tables and fields.

④ Click the Save button.

⑤ Type a name for the query. ⑥ Click OK.

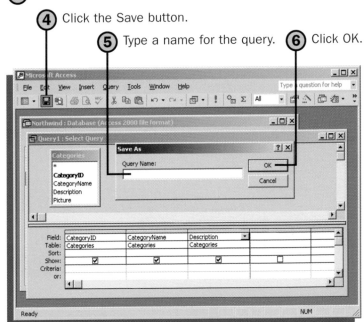

! **TIP:** To remove a table from the design grid, right-click the table's title bar and then click Remove Table.

Using Criteria to Focus Query Results

It's likely you won't want your query to find every record in a table—if you did, you could just open the table and not bother with the query! To limit the records a query locates, such as only finding customers in Germany, you can add criteria to the fields in the Query design grid.

! TIP: You can also type the criterion into the Criteria cell directly.

Set Query Criteria

1 Open a query in Design view.

3 Click the Build button.

4 Create the criterion in the Expression Builder.

5 Click OK.

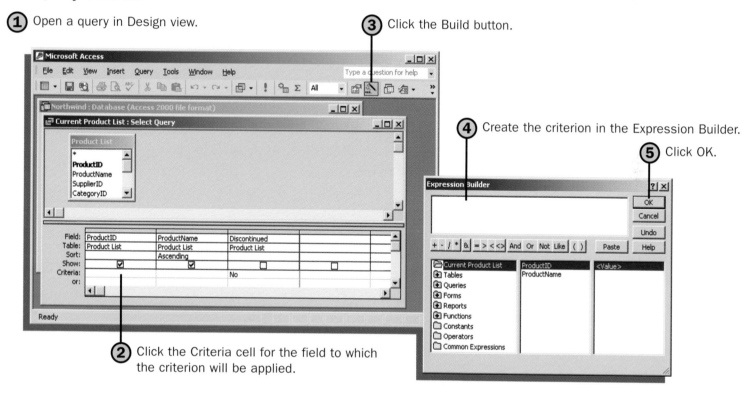

2 Click the Criteria cell for the field to which the criterion will be applied.

! TIP: To use a text string as a criterion, you should enclose the string in quotes (for example, "Germany"). If you forget, Access will add the quotes if it recognizes the criterion as a text string.

Introducing Operators

There are several types of database objects and tools you need to use when you create a criterion to narrow the records returned by a query or to calculate a value. The first set of objects to which you need to refer includes database tables and their fields. For example, to calculate the subtotal of a line in the Northwind sample database's Order Details table, you need to multiply the Unit Price by the Quantity ordered and adjust the total if the customer gets a discount (as noted in the Discount field). The expression to perform the first part of that calculation would be [Order Details]![UnitPrice]*[Order Details]![Quantity].

Note that table fields are called out with the name of the table enclosed in square brackets, an exclamation point, and then the name of the field in square brackets.

Arithmetic Operators

Operator	Description
-	Subtraction (6-4=2)
*	Multiplication (6*4=24)
/	Division (6/4=1.5)
\	Integer division (6\4=1)
+	Addition (6+4=10)
Mod	Modular division (6 Mod 4=2)

Comparison Operators

Operator	Description
<	Less than
<=	Less than or equal to
<>	Not equal to
=	Equals
>=	Greater than or equal to
>	Greater than
Between "Value1" And "Value2"	Between two values, inclusive (for example, Between "1" And "3" would return, "1, 2, 3")

Logical Operators

Operator	Description
AND	Both elements of an expression must be true.
NOT	The expression must evaluate as false.
OR	At least one element of an expression must be true.
XOR	Exactly one element of an expression must be true, not both.

Using Queries to Calculate Values

One popular use for database tables is to maintain sales records, with fields for the order identifier, the product ordered, and the product's price. What you can't do in a table is perform a calculation—the fields are just designed to hold data. In a query, however, you can find totals, averages, or even the minimum or maximum value in the records found by your query.

Calculate a Value in a Query

① Open a query in Design view.

② Click the Totals button to add the Total row to the query grid.

③ Click the Field cell in the column where you want to calculate the value.

Run button

④ Click the Build button.

⑤ Build the calculation in the Expression Builder.

⑥ Click OK.

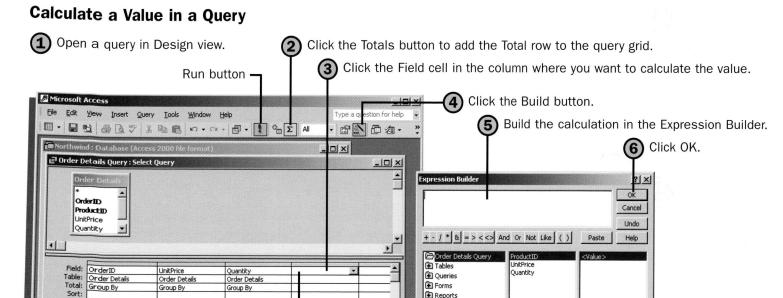

⑦ In the Field cell with the calculation, edit the value to the left of the colon to reflect the name you want for the field when the query results are displayed as a datasheet.

! **TIP:** To select fields from other tables for use in a calculation, double-click the Tables icon in the left pane of the Expression Builder, double-click the table with the target field, and then double-click the field name in the center pane.

⑧ Click the Run button.

! **TIP:** The fields used in the query appear in the middle pane of the Expression Builder.

Creating a Parameter Query

Some of the time, you can create a query that will always look for the same information, such as orders from a specific country or the total orders from an established customer. Other times, however, you and your colleagues need the flexibility to enter a criterion (such as a country) into the query to focus the results correctly. You can do that by creating a *parameter* query, which lets you specify the criteria the query uses to find records.

CAUTION: If you don't type a prompt between the square brackets, the only indication you'll get to enter a parameter is a blank dialog box. If a new colleague runs the query, he or she will have no idea what to type in the box!

Build a Parameter Query

1 Open a query in design view.

2 Type the prompt surrounded by square brackets in the Criteria cell in the column representing the field in which you want to find the entered value.

3 Click the Run button to test the query.

4 Type a value in the message box that appears.

5 Click OK.

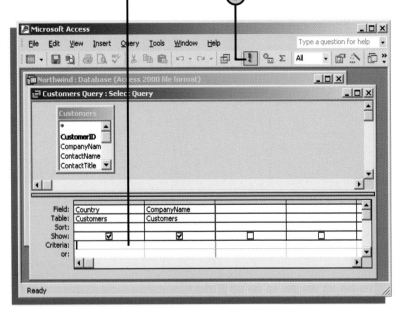

Finding Duplicate Records

The standard select query locates records that meet a criterion, such as orders made by a particular customer during a given month. However, you might also be interested in finding those customers who placed more than one order in a month. If all orders for a month were recorded in the same table, you could create a Find Duplicates query to locate CustomerID values that occur more than once in the table.

Create a Find Duplicates Query

① Click Queries on the Objects bar.

② Click New.

③ Click Find Duplicates Query Wizard.

④ Click OK.

⑤ Click the table in which you want to find duplicate information.

⑥ Click Next.

⑦ Click the field that might contain duplicate information.

⑧ Click Add.

⑨ Repeat steps 7–8 to add any other fields to the query.

⑩ Click Next.

⑪ Click any other field to display in the query results.

⑫ Click Add.

⑬ Repeat steps 11–12 as necessary.

⑭ Click Next.

⑮ Type a name for the query.

⑯ Click Finish.

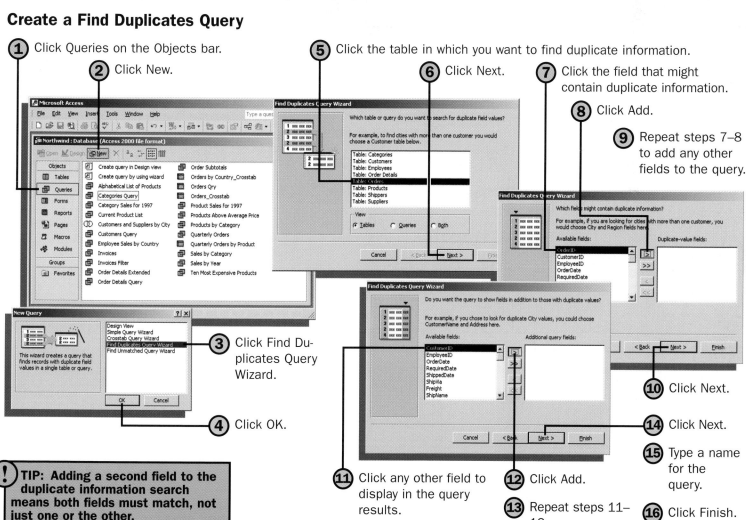

! TIP: Adding a second field to the duplicate information search means both fields must match, not just one or the other.

Finding Unmatched Records

When two tables are in a one-to-many relationship, you can create a Find Unmatched Records query to identify any records in the table on the "one" side that have no corresponding records in the table on the "many" side. For example, in the Northwind sample database, because the Customers and Orders tables are in a one-to-many relationship, you could identify customers that have never placed an order.

Create a Find Unmatched Records Query

① Click Queries on the Objects bar.

② Click New.

③ Click Find Unmatched Query Wizard.

④ Click OK.

⑤ Click the table in which you want to find unmatched records.

⑥ Click Next.

⑦ Click the table or query with related records.

⑧ Click Next.

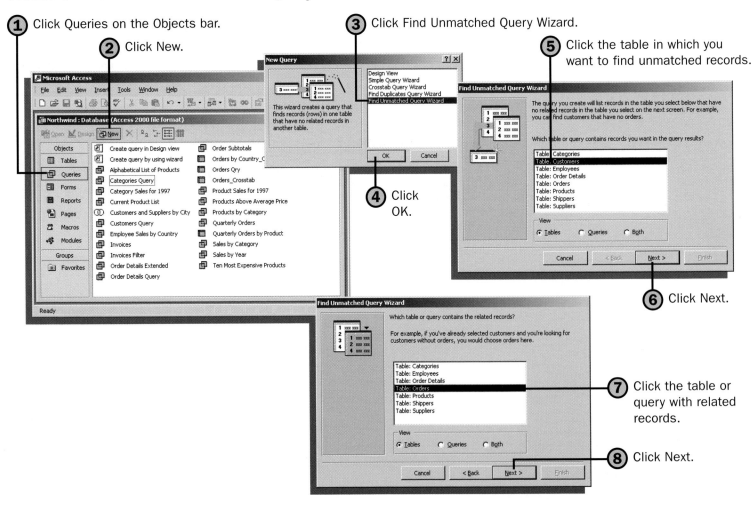

9 If necessary, click the field in the left pane that is in the table on the "one" side of the relationship.

10 If necessary, click the field in the right pane that is in the table on the "many" side of the relationship.

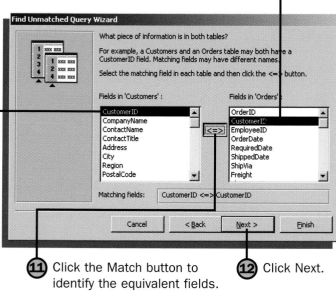

13 Click the name of a field to display in the query results.

14 Click Add.

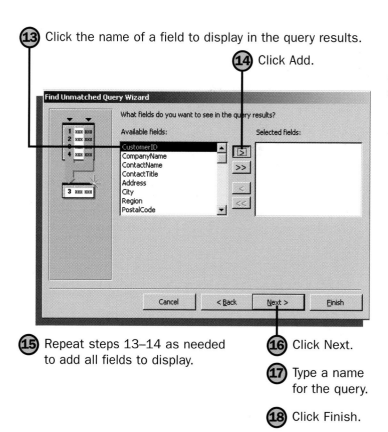

11 Click the Match button to identify the equivalent fields.

12 Click Next.

15 Repeat steps 13–14 as needed to add all fields to display.

16 Click Next.

17 Type a name for the query.

18 Click Finish.

TRY THIS: Open the Northwind sample database, click Queries on the Objects bar, and then click New. Click Find Unmatched Query Wizard, and then click OK. Click Table: Customers, and then click Next. In the next screen, click Table: Orders and then click Next. Verify that CustomerID is highlighted in both panes in the next screen, and click Next. Click Company Name, click the Add button, and then click Next. In the final screen, click Finish to accept the query name Access suggests. The query you created displays employee sales by country in a crosstab format.

Writing Query Results to a New Table

When you run a query, Access writes the records the query finds into a *dynaset*, or dynamic record set. While Access remembers the results of queries you've run, the results aren't actually written to a table, limiting what you can do with the data. You can, however, modify a select query so that the results are written to a new table.

Create a Make-Table Query

1 Open a query in Design view.

2 Choose Make-Table Query from the Query menu.

3 Type a name for the new table.

4 Click OK.

5 Click the Run button.

6 Click Yes to create the new table with the selected records.

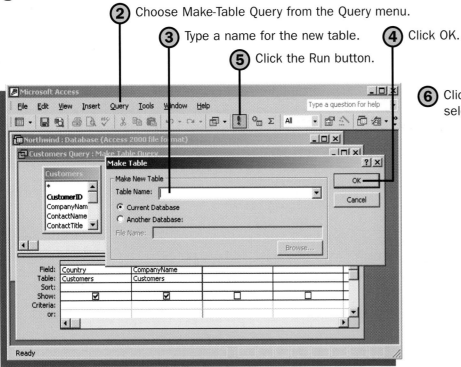

> **!** TIP: You can write the results of your query to a table in another database by selecting the Another Database option in the Make-Table Query dialog box, clicking the Browse button, and using the file navigation dialog box to identify the database to receive the table.

Creating an Update Query

One exciting aspect of business is how quickly things change—of course, it can be difficult to keep track of all those changes! One useful task you can perform with an Update query is to modify values in a table to reflect changes in your business environment. For example, if a supplier increases prices by 5 percent, you can create an Update query that moves through your Products table and updates the records for that supplier's products.

Update Table Values with a Query

① Open a query in Design view.

② Choose Update Query from the Query menu.

④ Click the Run button.

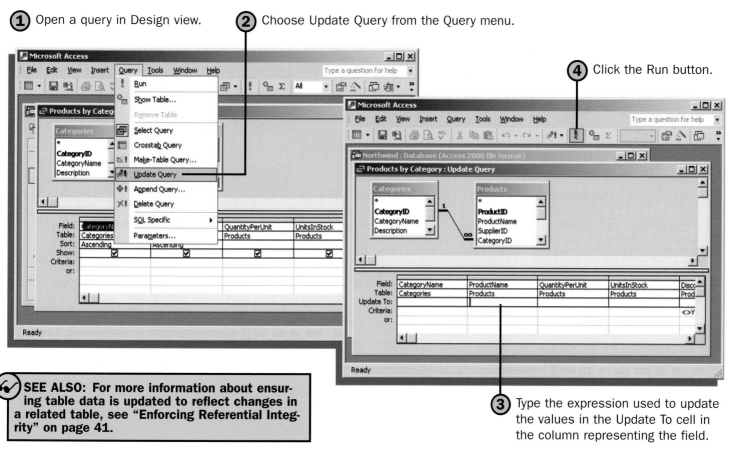

SEE ALSO: For more information about ensuring table data is updated to reflect changes in a related table, see "Enforcing Referential Integrity" on page 41.

③ Type the expression used to update the values in the Update To cell in the column representing the field.

Creating a Crosstab Query

The basic means of storing and presenting data in Access is the table, which is essentially a list of information about a group of "things" (such as customer orders) related to a single primary key value. Another way to present data is in a Crosstab query, which relates one value (such as a total or an average) with two other values (such as a customer and a month).

Build a Crosstab Query

(1) Click Queries on the Objects bar.

(2) Click New.

(3) Click Crosstab Query Wizard.

(5) Click the table to provide the values for your crosstab query.

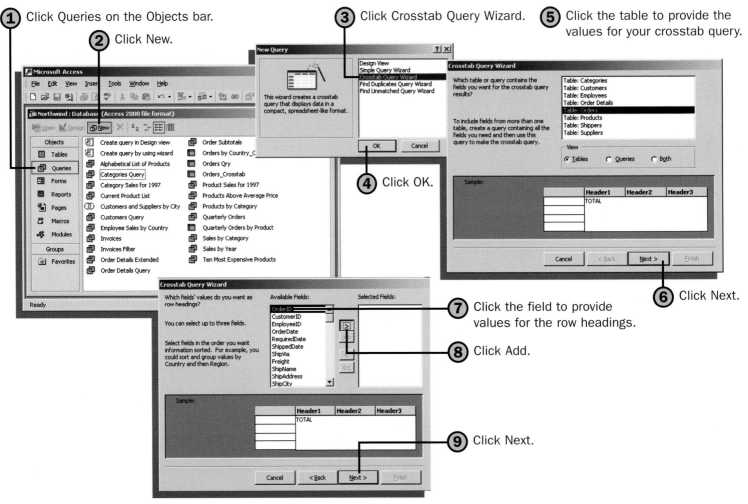

(4) Click OK.

(6) Click Next.

(7) Click the field to provide values for the row headings.

(8) Click Add.

(9) Click Next.

10 Click the field to provide values for the column headings.

12 Click the field to provide values for the data area (body) of the crosstab query.

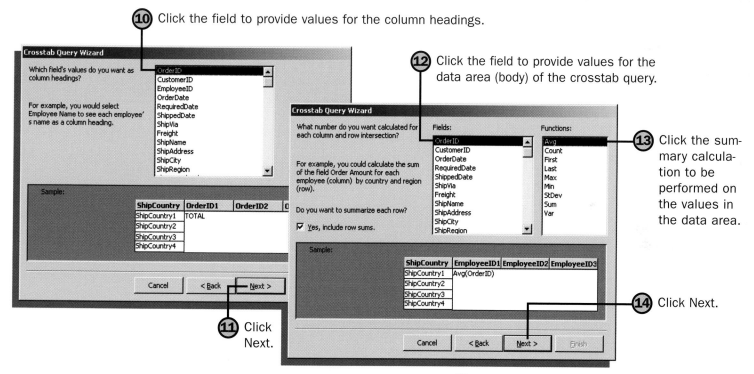

13 Click the summary calculation to be performed on the values in the data area.

11 Click Next.

14 Click Next.

15 Type a name for the query, and click Finish.

TRY THIS: Open the Northwind sample database, click Queries on the Objects bar, and then click New. Click Crosstab Query Wizard, and then click OK. Click Table: Orders, and then click Next. Click ShipCountry, click Add, and then click Next. Click EmployeeID, and then click Next. Click OrderID, click Count, and then click Next. Click Finish to accept the name Access suggests and to view the query's results. The query you created displays employee sales by country in a crosstab format.

SEE ALSO: For more information about using the power of spreadsheets to analyze Access data, see "Creating a PivotTable" on page 206.

9

Creating Reports

Reports give you the ability to present your table and query data in an accessible format. In some ways, reports and forms are very similar—both types of database objects let you display your table records and query results at one record per page, in a series of columns or rows, or in a custom layout you create in Design view. The difference between forms and reports is that in addition to *presenting* your table and query data, reports let you *summarize* your data. For example, you can create a report that not only lists every order made by every customer, but also finds the total amount of all orders for a particular customer. It's possible to do the same thing with queries, but the Report Wizard stream-lines the process greatly, saving you time and effort while producing valuable information.

In this chapter, you'll learn how to:

● Create a variety of reports using the Report Wizard.

● Create or modify an existing form in Design view.

● Add, remove, and edit report controls.

● Calculate values in a report.

● Create a subreport.

● Print address labels from table or query data.

Creating a Report Using the Report Wizard

While it might be possible to generate useful reports from the data in a single table or query, it's very likely that you'll want to combine data from more than one table or query into a single report. For example, you might have product data in one table and supplier data in another table, and then want to create a report where full supplier contact information accompanies the product information. You can do that by creating a report using the Report Wizard.

Step Through the Report Wizard

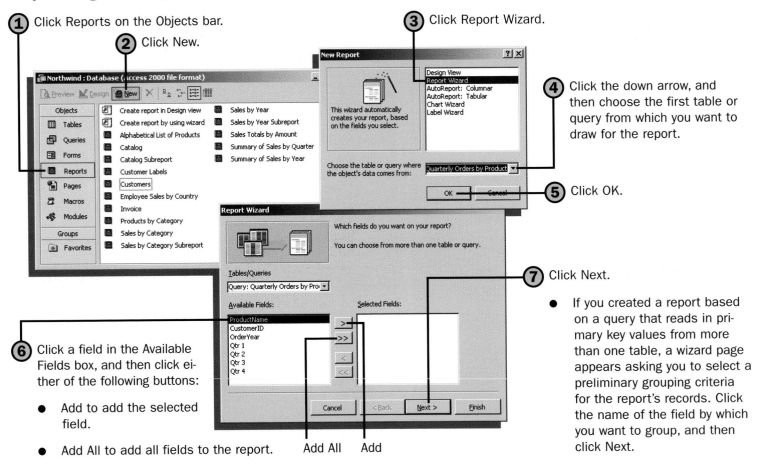

1 Click Reports on the Objects bar.

2 Click New.

3 Click Report Wizard.

4 Click the down arrow, and then choose the first table or query from which you want to draw for the report.

5 Click OK.

6 Click a field in the Available Fields box, and then click either of the following buttons:

- Add to add the selected field.

- Add All to add all fields to the report.

Add All   Add

7 Click Next.

- If you created a report based on a query that reads in primary key values from more than one table, a wizard page appears asking you to select a preliminary grouping criteria for the report's records. Click the name of the field by which you want to group, and then click Next.

8 If necessary, click the first field by which you want to group the report's contents, and then click Add. Repeat to add additional grouping levels.

10 Click the first field's down arrow, and click the first field by which you want to sort the report's contents.

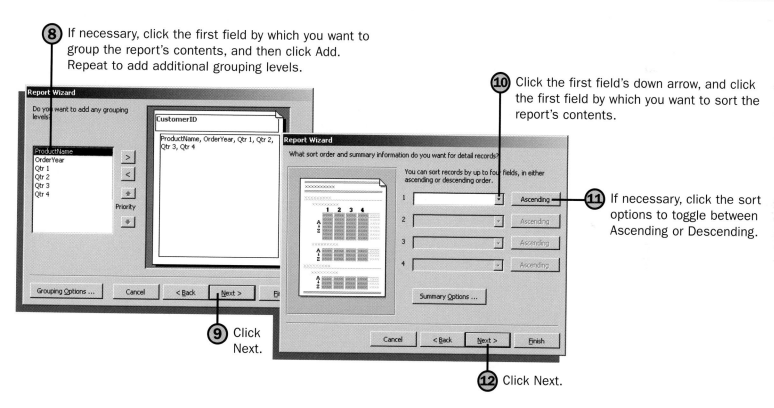

9 Click Next.

11 If necessary, click the sort options to toggle between Ascending or Descending.

12 Click Next.

13 Use the controls on the remaining wizard pages to select a layout, page orientation, style, and name for the report. When you're done, click Finish.

SEE ALSO: For information about changing report grouping levels, see "Grouping Report Records" on page 111.

Creating a Summary Report

Although both database object types let you display your table and query records, one thing you can do in a report that you can't with a form is to summarize your data within a report. For example, if you created a summary report of all orders and grouped the report's contents by product, you could add a summary function to find the total sales for each product. You could also find the minimum, maximum, or average value of orders for each listed product.

Build a Summary Report

① Click Reports on the Objects bar.

② Click New.

③ Click Report Wizard.

④ Click the down arrow, and click the table or query to serve as the base for the report.

⑤ Click OK.

⑥ Click a field in the Available Fields box and then click either of the following buttons:

- Add to add the selected field to the report.

- Add All to add every field to the report.

⑦ When you're done adding fields, click Next.

- If you created a report based on a query that reads in primary key values from more than one table, a wizard page appears asking you to select a preliminary grouping criteria for the report's records. Click the name of the table by which you want to group, and then click Next.

SEE ALSO: For information about changing report grouping levels, see "Grouping Report Records" on page 111.

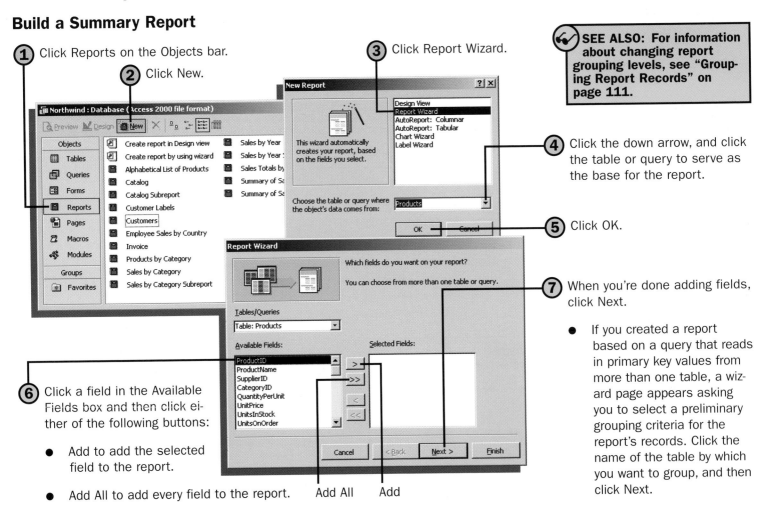

Add All   Add

8 Click the first field by which you want to group the report's contents, and then click Add. Repeat to add additional grouping levels.

9 Click Next.

> **! TIP: You can select more than one field and summary function— every summary you choose will appear in your finished report.**

10 Click the first field's down arrow, and click the first field by which you want to sort the report's contents.

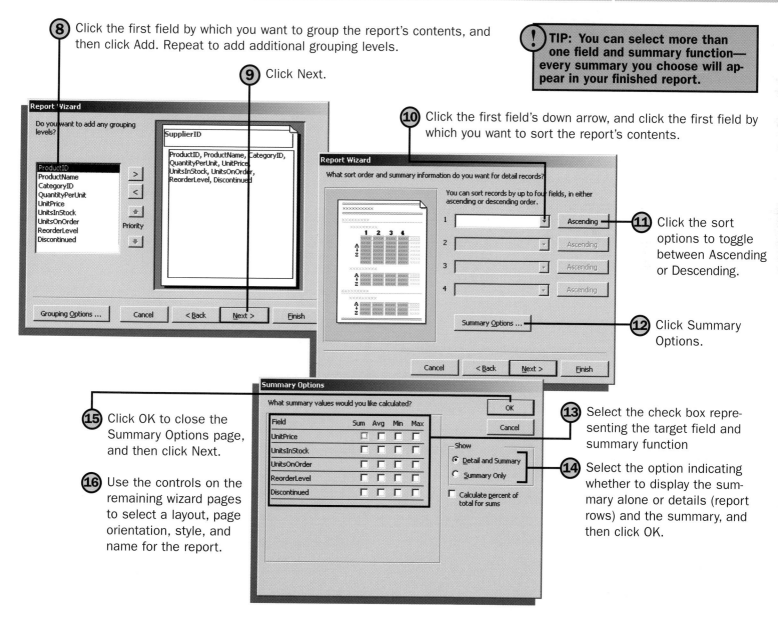

11 Click the sort options to toggle between Ascending or Descending.

12 Click Summary Options.

15 Click OK to close the Summary Options page, and then click Next.

16 Use the controls on the remaining wizard pages to select a layout, page orientation, style, and name for the report.

13 Select the check box representing the target field and summary function

14 Select the option indicating whether to display the summary alone or details (report rows) and the summary, and then click OK.

Understanding Report Types

As with forms, you have a great deal of flexibility in choosing how to create a report and what the report should look like when you're done. The first set of options is presented to you in the New Report dialog box.

AutoReports, as the name suggests, are simple reports that Microsoft Access creates from a single table or query. In a Columnar AutoReport, table fields are represented as rows, with each instance of the object represented by the table described by the values in a column. In a Tabular AutoReport, table fields are represented as columns, and each instance of the table object is described by the values in a complete set of rows.

If you want to limit the fields that contribute to a report's contents or to create reports that draw values from more than one table or query, you can run the Report Wizard. In the Report Wizard, you can add fields from any table or query, choose how to arrange the report's results, and determine a look for the report.

Click to build a report from scratch.

Click to build a report using the wizard.

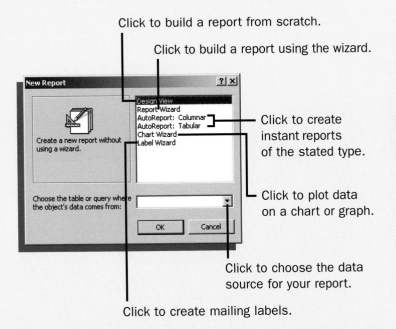

Click to create instant reports of the stated type.

Click to plot data on a chart or graph.

Click to choose the data source for your report.

Click to create mailing labels.

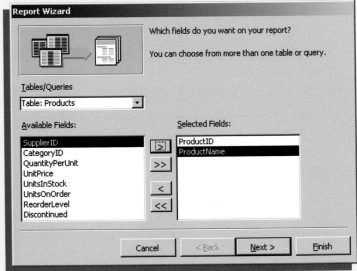

Creating a Report in Design View

The AutoReport wizards and the Report Wizard make it easy to create reports, but you can also create a blank form in Design view and start adding controls on your own. If the report will consist only of a few fields and you want to place the fields in particular locations, you might want to create the report in Design view, rather than creating it using a wizard and then editing the result in Design view. Of course, you may just prefer working in Design view!

Build a New Report

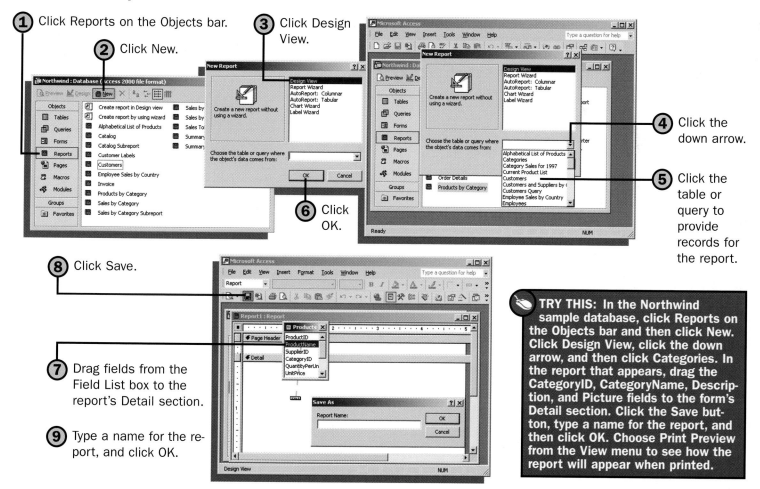

(1) Click Reports on the Objects bar.

(2) Click New.

(3) Click Design View.

(4) Click the down arrow.

(5) Click the table or query to provide records for the report.

(6) Click OK.

(7) Drag fields from the Field List box to the report's Detail section.

(8) Click Save.

(9) Type a name for the report, and click OK.

> **TRY THIS:** In the Northwind sample database, click Reports on the Objects bar and then click New. Click Design View, click the down arrow, and then click Categories. In the report that appears, drag the CategoryID, CategoryName, Description, and Picture fields to the form's Detail section. Click the Save button, type a name for the report, and then click OK. Choose Print Preview from the View menu to see how the report will appear when printed.

Modifying an Existing Report

Once you've created a report, you can open it in Design view and add or remove fields. The available fields will appear in the Field List box; to add a field, just drag its name from the Field List box to the body of the report.

Open a Report for Editing

③ Click Design to open the report in Design view.

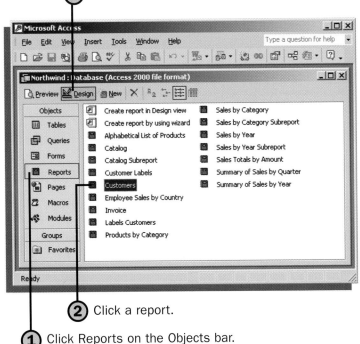

② Click a report.

① Click Reports on the Objects bar.

Display or Hide the Field List

① Click the Field List button to display the Field List box.

② Click the Close box to hide the Field List box.

Add a Field to a Report

① Drag the field from the Field List box to the desired spot on the form.

Field List button

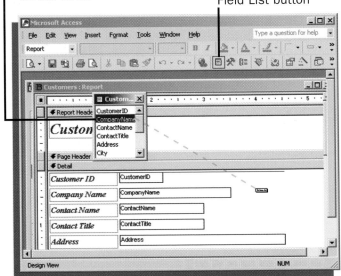

✔ **SEE ALSO:** For more information about modifying reports, see Chapter 10, "Beautifying Forms and Reports."

① TIP: When you have a report open in Design view, you can also display the Field List box by pressing F8.

Adding and Deleting Report Controls

After you've created a report, you can add controls such as labels, text boxes, check boxes, and option buttons to display your table and query data. The specific steps you take to add a control and define its data source depend on the control you want to create, but the Control wizards are there to help you through the process.

When you create a control, you actually create a control (such as a text box) *and* a label identifying the control. You can delete, modify, or move the label without affecting its associated control.

Add a Control Using a Wizard

① Open a report in Design view.

② If necessary, click the Toolbox button.

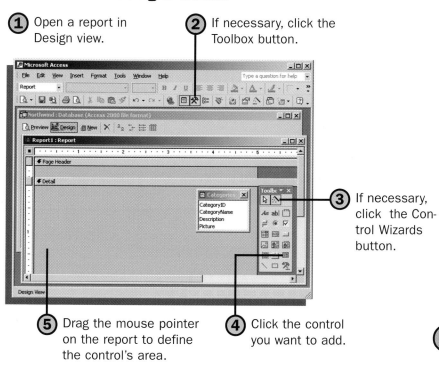

③ If necessary, click the Control Wizards button.

⑤ Drag the mouse pointer on the report to define the control's area.

④ Click the control you want to add.

⑥ Follow the steps in the wizard to define the contents of the control.

Delete a Control

① Click the control you want to delete.

② Click the Cut button.

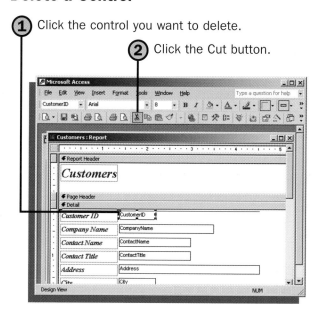

! **TIP: When deleting a control, be sure to click the control itself—not the label next to the control.**

! **TIP: You can change the value in a control's label by editing the label directly or by setting the control's Caption property.**

Modify Control Properties

① Click the control. ② Click the Properties button.

SEE ALSO: For more information about controls and control types, see the table "Available Control Types" on page 76.

③ Click the property to change.

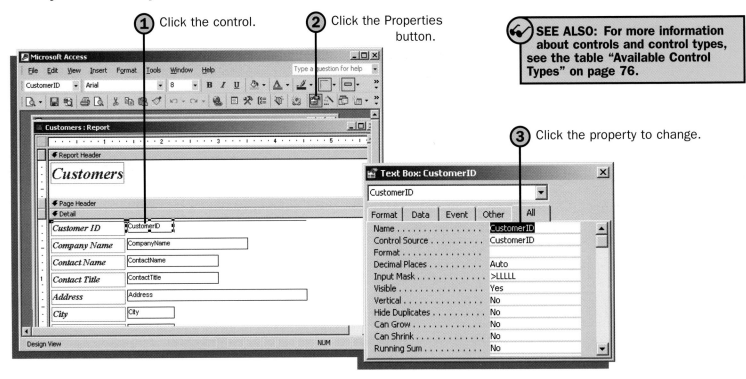

④ Follow one of these steps:

- Type a new value in the text box next to the property name.

- Click the down arrow, and select a new property from the list that appears.

- Click the Build button, and use the dialog box that appears to select or construct a new value.

Calculating Values in a Report

When you create a report, you can create a control (such as a text box) that performs a calculation on the values elsewhere in the report. For example, if a report record had a field for a product's price and another field noting the quantity ordered, you could create a control that multiplies the values from those fields and displays the result. Creating calculated fields in a report is handy when you are working with a popular query and you don't want Access to recalculate the values every time the query is run.

SEE ALSO: For information about calculating summary values in a report, as opposed to calculating a value based on the current record, see "Creating a Summary Report" on page 102.

Create a Calculated Field

1 Open a report in Design view.

2 If necessary, click the Toolbox button.

TIP: Clicking the Build button to the right of the Control Source property opens the Expression Builder.

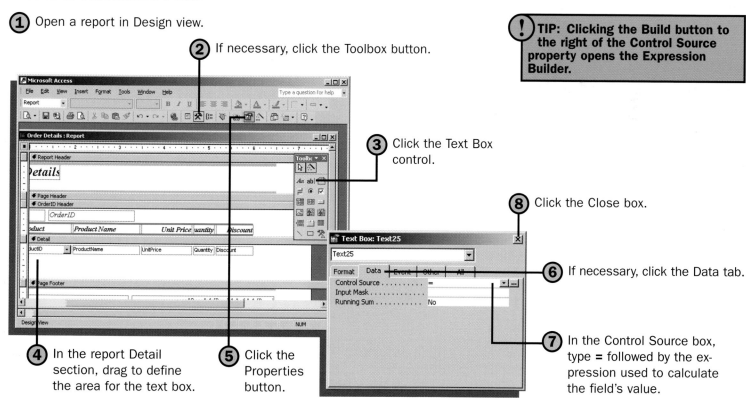

3 Click the Text Box control.

8 Click the Close box.

6 If necessary, click the Data tab.

7 In the Control Source box, type = followed by the expression used to calculate the field's value.

4 In the report Detail section, drag to define the area for the text box.

5 Click the Properties button.

Introducing Report Sections

A basic report has five sections:

- Report Header

- Page Header

- Report Footer

- Page Footer

- Detail

The Report Header section holds information that appears at the top of the first page of the printed report. Typical information you'd find in the Report Header includes the title of the report, the logo of the company producing the report, and the report's author.

The Page Header, by contrast, contains information that appears at the top of every printed report page. Most frequently you'll find page numbers and dates in this report area, but you could also put smaller versions of a company logo in this area to identify the report's origins. If the report data is confidential, this area (and the Report Header or Footer) is a good place to note that, as the annotation would appear on every page.

The Page Footer and Report Footer sections are the complement of the Page Header and Report Header sections. Information in the Page Footer section appears at the bottom of every printed report page, while information in the Report Footer section appears at the bottom of the last printed report page.

The report's Detail section is where the table records or query results appear. Whether the Detail section has a one or more than one record depends on how you set up your report. As with any report section, you can add other controls, text, or drawing objects to make your data easier to comprehend.

If you add a grouping level to a report, Access lets you add a header and footer section named after the field used to group the report's contents. For example, if you were to group the contents of a report based on a query combining data from the Customers, Orders, and Order Details tables, you could group the report's contents by the country of the customer. If you did, two sections named Country Header and Country Footer would appear in the report, flanking the Detail section.

Grouping Report Records

When you create a report using the Report Wizard, you can define how the report's records will be grouped. For example, you could create a report based on the Northwind sample database's Order and Order Details tables and group records by CustomerID. If you wanted to display each customer's orders by the date they were placed, you could create a second grouping level based on the OrderDate field.

When you add a grouping level to a report, Access adds a header and footer corresponding to the grouping field's name. If you grouped a set of products by their category name, Access would create a CategoryName Header and a CategoryName Footer.

Create a Grouping Level

1 Open a report in Design view.

2 Click the Sorting And Grouping button.

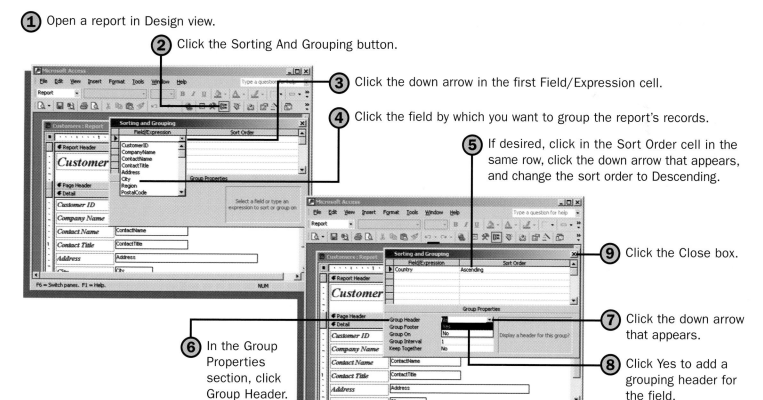

3 Click the down arrow in the first Field/Expression cell.

4 Click the field by which you want to group the report's records.

5 If desired, click in the Sort Order cell in the same row, click the down arrow that appears, and change the sort order to Descending.

9 Click the Close box.

6 In the Group Properties section, click Group Header.

7 Click the down arrow that appears.

8 Click Yes to add a grouping header for the field.

Reorder Grouping Levels

① Open a report in Design view.

② Click the Sorting And Grouping button.

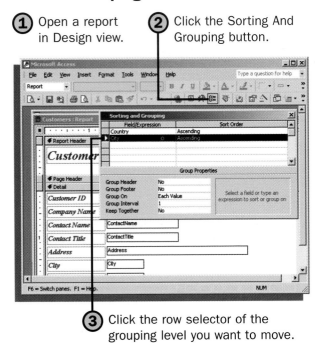

③ Click the row selector of the grouping level you want to move.

④ Drag the row selector to the desired position in the dialog box.

Delete a Grouping Level

① Open the report in Design view.

② Click the Sorting And Grouping button.

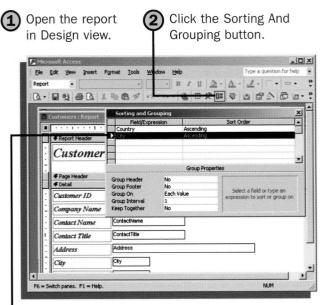

③ Click the row selector of the grouping level you want to delete.

④ Press Delete.

⑤ Click Yes to confirm you want to delete the grouping level and any associated report sections.

Creating a Subreport

An Access database often has a number of relationships between tables. In the Northwind sample database, for example, Suppliers make Products, which are part of Orders placed by Customers. When two tables are in a one-to-many relationship, you can create a report based on the contents of the table on the "one" side of the relationship and add a subreport displaying related records from the table on the "many" side of the relationship. The Customers and Orders tables are in a one-to-many relationship (they have the CustomerID field in common), so you could create a report listing every customer and add a subreport displaying all orders placed by the current customer.

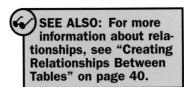

SEE ALSO: For more information about relationships, see "Creating Relationships Between Tables" on page 40.

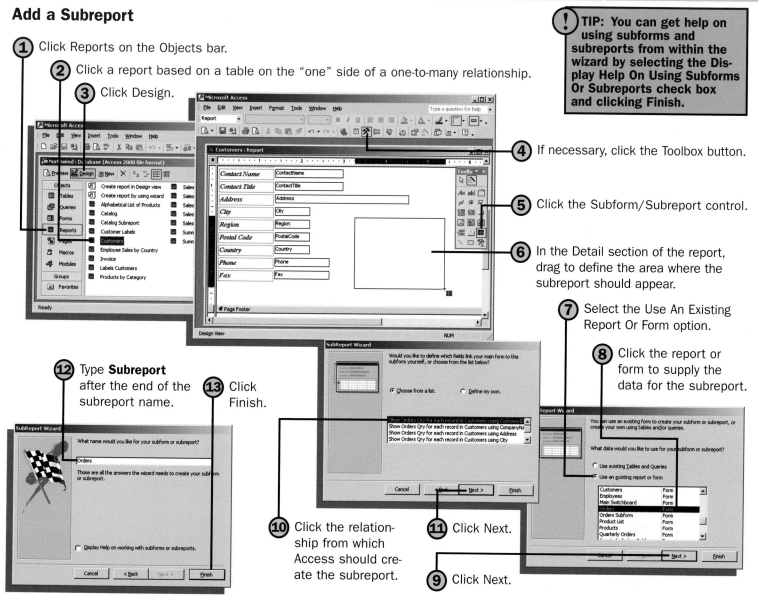

Add a Subreport

(1) Click Reports on the Objects bar.

(2) Click a report based on a table on the "one" side of a one-to-many relationship.

(3) Click Design.

(4) If necessary, click the Toolbox button.

(5) Click the Subform/Subreport control.

(6) In the Detail section of the report, drag to define the area where the subreport should appear.

(7) Select the Use An Existing Report Or Form option.

(8) Click the report or form to supply the data for the subreport.

(9) Click Next.

(10) Click the relationship from which Access should create the subreport.

(11) Click Next.

(12) Type **Subreport** after the end of the subreport name.

(13) Click Finish.

> **TIP: You can get help on using subforms and subreports from within the wizard by selecting the Display Help On Using Subforms Or Subreports check box and clicking Finish.**

Creating Mailing Labels

One frequent use for contact information in a database is to create a set of mailing labels so you can send special offers or notes of appreciation to all or a subset of your customers or suppliers. The Label Wizard walks you through the process, letting you choose the type of label you'll be printing, pick the table and query fields you want printed on the labels, and add any punctuation or other text to each label.

Generate Mailing Labels

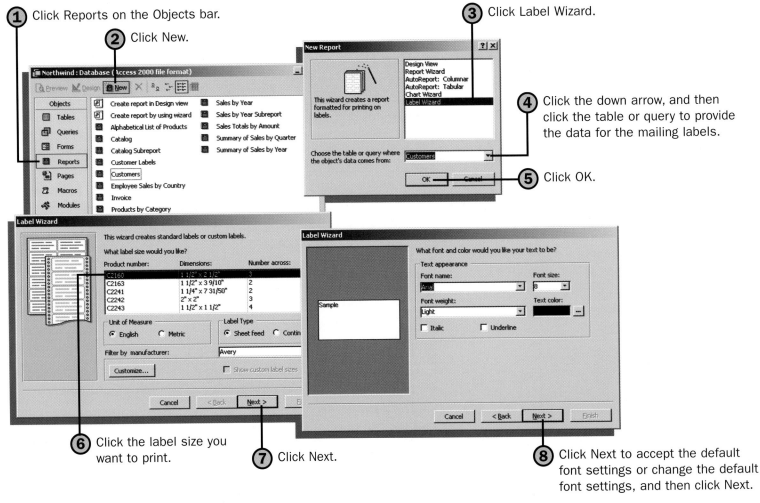

① Click Reports on the Objects bar.

② Click New.

③ Click Label Wizard.

④ Click the down arrow, and then click the table or query to provide the data for the mailing labels.

⑤ Click OK.

⑥ Click the label size you want to print.

⑦ Click Next.

⑧ Click Next to accept the default font settings or change the default font settings, and then click Next.

⑨ Click the first field to appear on the label.

⑩ Click the Add button.

TIP: Line breaks aren't accepted in the Label Wizard. To position text on the label's next line, click the line.

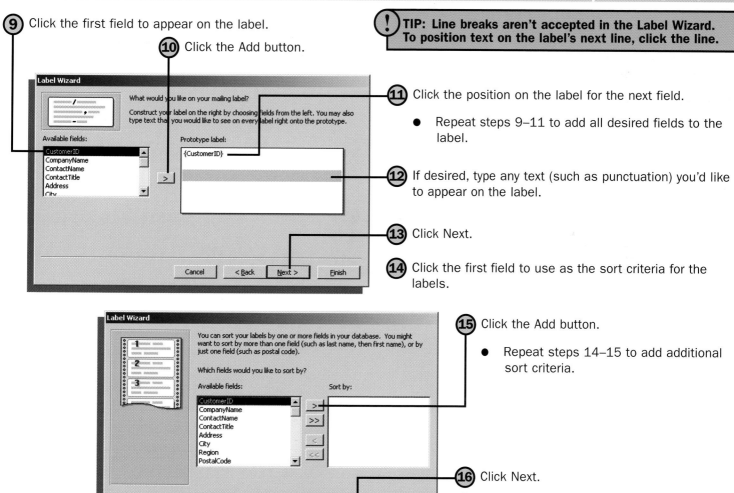

⑪ Click the position on the label for the next field.

- Repeat steps 9–11 to add all desired fields to the label.

⑫ If desired, type any text (such as punctuation) you'd like to appear on the label.

⑬ Click Next.

⑭ Click the first field to use as the sort criteria for the labels.

⑮ Click the Add button.

- Repeat steps 14–15 to add additional sort criteria.

⑯ Click Next.

⑰ Type a name for the report, and click Finish.

SEE ALSO: For more information about how grouping and sorting affect the order of records on a report, see "Grouping Report Records" on page 111.

TIP: You should always print one page of mailing labels on regular paper to be sure everything lines up correctly and looks the way you want it to.

10 Beautifying Forms and Reports

Once you've created forms and reports to display your table and query data, you can change the appearance of any control on the form or report. You can change the appearance of individual elements in your Microsoft Access objects, but an easier way to change the format of an entire document at once is to use an AutoFormat. You can use an AutoFormat as it is "out of the box" or you can choose to apply certain parts of the AutoFormat. If you want, you can even create and modify your own AutoFormats so that you can make the appearance of your forms and reports consistent.

Another useful Access feature is a conditional format, which changes the appearance of the data in a text box based on the data's value. If a customer hasn't placed an order in the last year, a product has been discontinued, or a shipment took more than a week to arrive, you can use conditional formats to highlight that data and bring it to your attention quickly.

In this chapter, you'll learn how to:

● Format the text on your forms and reports.

● Apply, create, and modify AutoFormats.

● Change the appearance of form and report controls.

● Add and edit lines, shapes, and borders.

● Define and apply conditional formats.

Formatting Text

Access is a great program for storing your data efficiently, but it also gives you a lot of flexibility in choosing how to display data in forms and reports. One important part of designing a form or report is choosing formats for each element of the design: labels, headings, and data. Corporate logos, color schemes, and documents can help guide initial development, but you should always listen to your colleagues to discover ways to make the text on your forms and reports easier to understand. Opening a form or report in Design view lets you make your changes, but feel free to switch between Design view and either Form view (for forms) or Print Preview (for reports) to see how your changes will look in the finished document.

Change Text Formatting

1 Select the text to be formatted.

2 Use the buttons on the Formatting (Form/Report) toolbar to format your text.

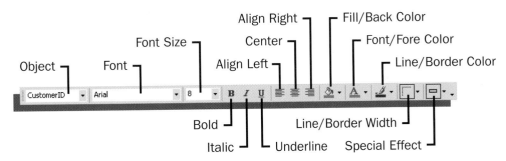

TIP: You can also view and change an object's appearance by clicking the object, clicking the Properties button, clicking the Format tab, and setting the image's formatting properties. For more information, see page 138.

Applying AutoFormats

Rather than define the format of every object in your forms and reports, you can apply one of the AutoFormats installed with Access. AutoFormats let you do more than just apply an existing format, however; you can choose which elements of an AutoFormat to apply, create new AutoFormats to match the formatting of an existing form or report, or modify an existing AutoFormat.

Select an AutoFormat

1 Open the report or form you want to format in Design view.

2 Choose AutoFormat from the Format menu.

3 Click the format you want to apply to your form or report.

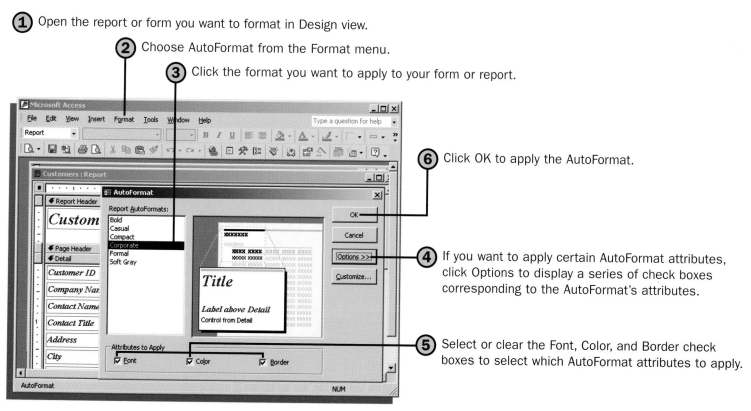

6 Click OK to apply the AutoFormat.

4 If you want to apply certain AutoFormat attributes, click Options to display a series of check boxes corresponding to the AutoFormat's attributes.

5 Select or clear the Font, Color, and Border check boxes to select which AutoFormat attributes to apply.

Customize an AutoFormat

① Open the report or form you want to format in Design view.

② Choose AutoFormat from the Format menu.

③ Click the AutoFormat you want to customize.

✋ **CAUTION:** While you can delete and modify the included AutoFormats, you should probably create a new AutoFormat based on an existing AutoFormat and modify the copy.

④ Click Customize.

⑤ Select the Update option to modify the selected AutoFormat to match the formatting of the active form or report.

⑥ Click OK to close the Customize AutoFormat dialog box.

⑦ Click OK to close the AutoFormat dialog box.

Create an AutoFormat

1 Open the report or form with the proper formatting in Design view.

2 Choose AutoFormat from the Format menu.

TIP: To delete an AutoFormat, open the AutoFormat dialog box, click the AutoFormat to delete, click Customize, select the Delete option, and then click OK.

3 Click Customize.

4 Select the Create A New AutoFormat option.

5 Type the name of the new AutoFormat in the New Style Name dialog box.

6 Click OK.

7 Click OK to close the AutoFormat dialog box.

Setting Control Appearance

Once you've added controls to a form or report, you can change the appearance of those controls using the buttons on the Formatting (Form/Report) toolbar. You can change the color of any control element as well as apply special effects to the controls, changing how they're drawn on the form or report. You can also use the Format menu's commands to arrange and distribute your controls attractively.

Change Control Colors

① Click the control you want to format.

② Follow any of these steps:

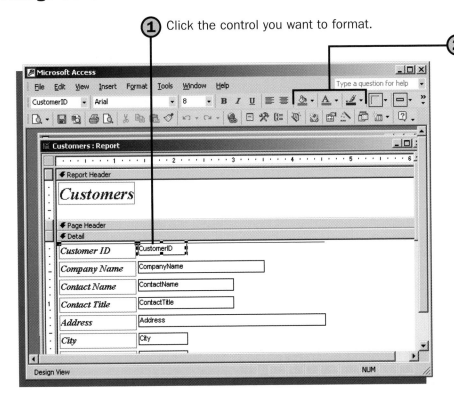

- Click the Fill/Back Color button's down arrow, and choose a color for the control's background elements.

- Click the Font/Fore Color button's down arrow, and choose a color for the control's foreground and text elements.

- Click the Line/Border Color button's down arrow, and choose a color for the control's lines and borders.

Format Controls with Special Effects

① Click the control you want to format.

② Click the Special Effects button's down arrow.

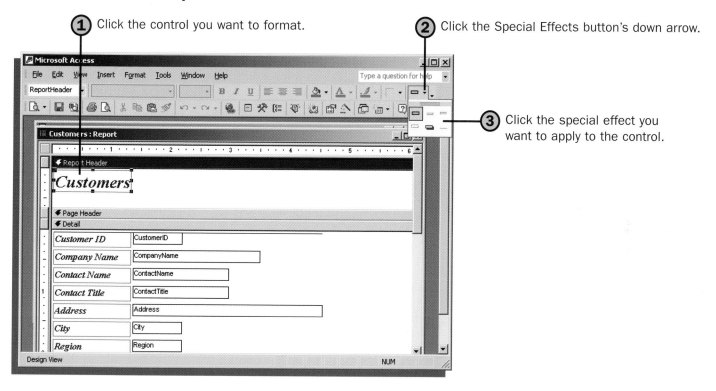

③ Click the special effect you want to apply to the control.

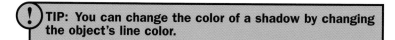

TIP: You can change the color of a shadow by changing the object's line color.

CAUTION: Applying the Etched and Chiseled special effects removes an object's fill and line/border color settings.

Distribute Controls Horizontally

1 Select the controls you want to distribute on the form or report.

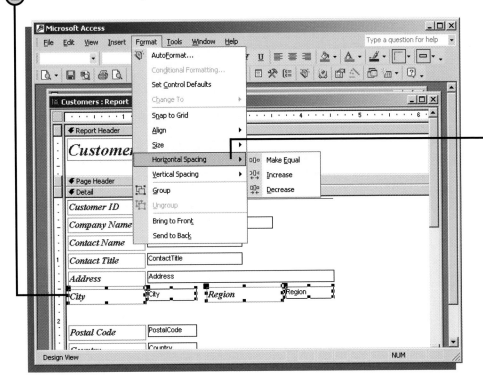

2 Point to Horizontal Spacing on the Format menu, and then follow any of these steps:

- Click Make Equal to place the controls the same distance apart from each other.

- Click Increase to increase the distance between the controls.

- Click Decrease to decrease the distance between the controls.

TIP: It's usually a good idea to start with your controls a uniform distance apart, so you should consider clicking Make Equal before using the Increase or Decrease options to change the layout of your controls.

Distribute Controls Vertically

① Select the controls you want to distribute on the form or report.

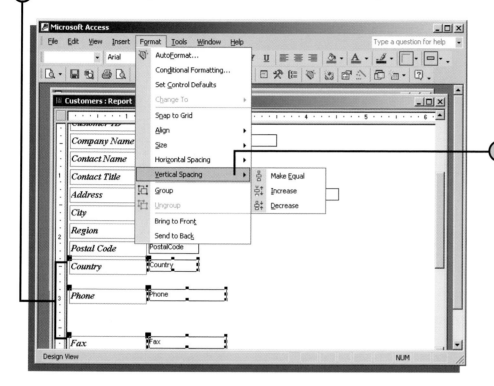

② Point to Vertical Spacing on the Format menu, and then follow any of these steps:

- Click Make Equal to place the controls the same distance apart from each other.

- Click Increase to increase the distance between the controls.

- Click Decrease to decrease the distance between the controls.

TRY THIS: Open the Northwind sample database, click Forms on the Objects bar, click Products, and then click Design. Select the Product ID, Product Name, Supplier, and Category labels. Point to Vertical Spacing on the Format menu, and click Decrease. The labels will move closer together. To return the labels to their previous spacing, point to Vertical Spacing on the Format menu and click Increase. Click the Close box to close the form.

Align Controls

1 Select the controls you want to align.

2 Point to Align on the Format menu, and then click the alignment you want to apply to the selected controls.

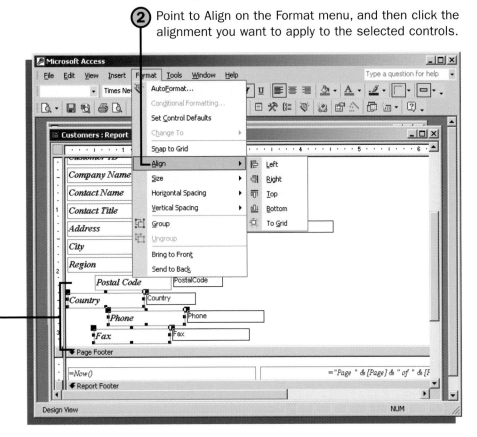

- Click Left to align the selected objects by their left edges.

- Click Right to align the selected objects by their right edges.

- Click Top to align the selected objects by their top edges.

- Click Bottom to align the selected objects by their bottom edges.

- Click To Grid to move each object to the nearest point on the design grid.

! TIP: If you want to help ensure that your objects will be aligned, you can choose Snap To Grid from the Format menu to turn on the grid. Turning on the grid limits where you can place your objects; if you want to place an object so it isn't aligned with the design grid, hold down the Ctrl key while you move the object.

! TIP: For even more control over your form and report controls' appearance, click the control you want to modify, click the Properties button, click the Format tab, and set the properties using the tools in the Properties box.

Adding Lines, Shapes, and Borders

When you create a control to display form and report data, you also create a label that you can modify to identify the data presented in the control. While labels are a great help in identifying the source of your form and report data, they only go so far in identifying groups of controls. For example, if you were to create a report from the contents of a Products table, you could separate general information about a product (such as its category and supplier) from the more specific information by drawing a line between the two groups of controls.

Draw a Line

1 If necessary, click the Toolbox button.

2 Click the Line control.

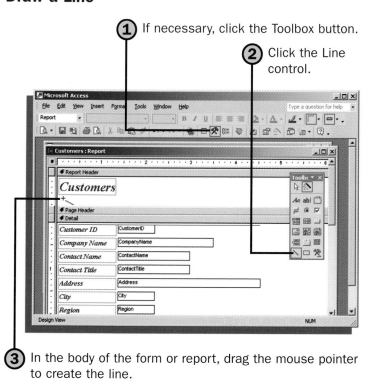

3 In the body of the form or report, drag the mouse pointer to create the line.

Draw a Shape

1 If necessary, click the Toolbox button.

2 Click the Rectangle control.

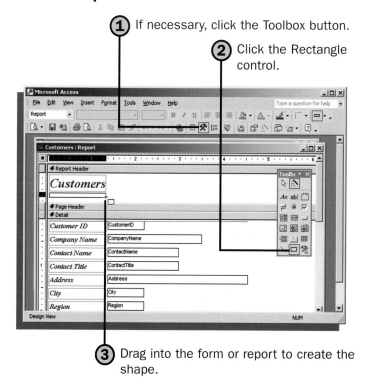

3 Drag into the form or report to create the shape.

Add a Border

1 In Design view, click the object to which you want to apply the border.

2 Click the Line/Border Width button's down arrow.

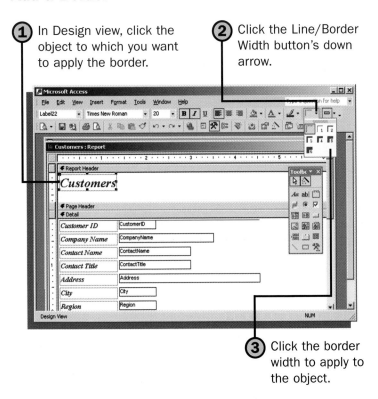

3 Click the border width to apply to the object.

Change an Object's Fill Color

1 Click the object you want to edit.

2 Click the Fill/Back Color button's down arrow.

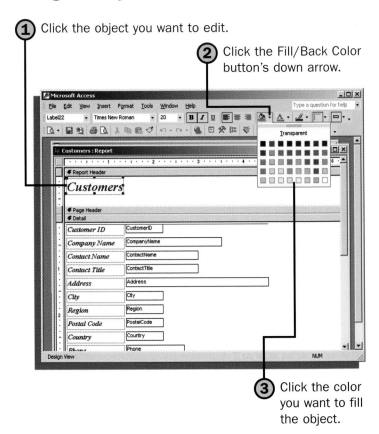

3 Click the color you want to fill the object.

! TIP: In Design view, objects have lines drawn around them to indicate their real size, so they may appear to have a border when they don't. If you're not sure, view the form in Form view or a report in Preview to see if there is a border.

Editing Lines and Borders

Once you've added a line to a form or report, or displayed a border around a control, you can change the properties of the line or border. You can move, resize, or change the color of a line, and change the color of a border.

Resize a Line

(1) Click either end of the line you want to resize.

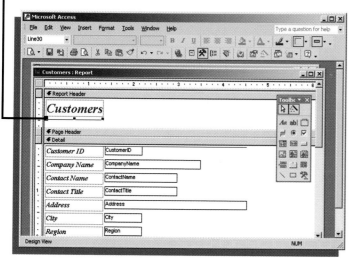

(2) Drag any of the handles surrounding the line to resize the line.

> **!** TIP: Dragging the handle at either end of the line lets you move that end of the line freely.

Change Line and Border Color

(1) Click the line or object you want to change.

(2) Click the Line/Border Color button's down arrow.

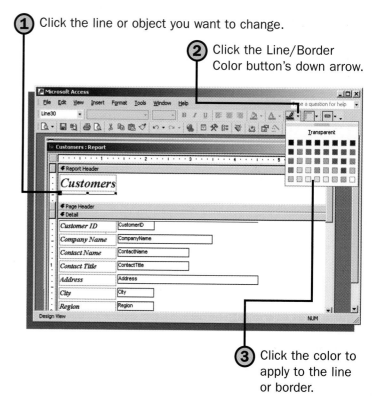

(3) Click the color to apply to the line or border.

> **!** TIP: You can repeat your last color selection by clicking the Line/Border Color button—the most recently used color appears on the button's face.

Adding a Picture

The old saying that "a picture is worth a thousand words" is often true—a photograph of a product or a diagram of a process can provide valuable contextual information to help you and your colleagues understand form and report data. Also, whether you work for yourself or for a large company, it's important to add your logo to any documents you want to distribute outside your organization.

Another important consideration when adding a picture to an Access object is whether to embed the picture in the file, which increases the database file's size every time you use the picture, or to link to a single copy of the picture that travels everywhere with the database. If you use the image frequently, or if it's a large file, you should change the embedded image to a linked image.

Embed a Picture

1 Open a form or report in Design view.

2 Choose Picture from the Insert menu.

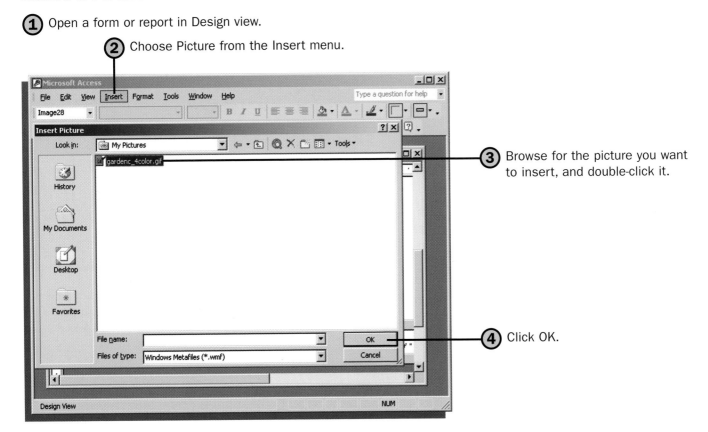

3 Browse for the picture you want to insert, and double-click it.

4 Click OK.

Change an Embedded Picture to a Linked Picture

(1) Open the form or report containing the picture in Design view.

(2) Click the embedded picture.

(3) Click the Properties button.

SEE ALSO: For information about adding borders to your pictures, see "Adding Lines, Shapes, and Borders" on page 127.

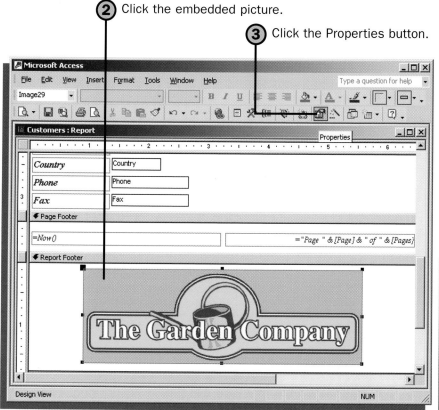

(4) If necessary, click the Format tab.

(5) Click the Picture Type box.

(6) Click the down arrow.

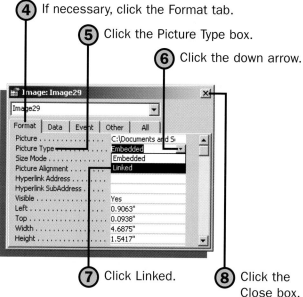

(7) Click Linked.

(8) Click the Close box.

Applying Conditional Formatting

Changing the appearance of your form and report data by applying formats (or AutoFormats) makes your data easier to read. However, you may want to apply different formats to a control's contents based on the data's value. For example, you might want to highlight the names of any customers who are within 10 percent of their credit limit or display information about discontinued products in red.

✋ **CAUTION:** If you change the appearance of a control's contents by making the contents bold or increasing the font size, be sure the control is large enough to display the data.

Define a Conditional Format

1 Click the text box to which you want to apply a conditional format.

2 Choose Conditional Formatting from the Format menu.

3 Use the controls in the Default Formatting area to define a format to be applied if no conditions are met.

ⓘ **TIP:** If you create multiple conditions, make sure there is no overlap between the conditions, such as one condition checking if a number is less than 3000 and another checking if the same number is less than 1500. If there is overlap, the first condition Access checks will be applied. The proper way to create the conditions would be to check in Condition 1 if a value is between 1500 and 3000 and then check in Condition 2 if the value is less than 1500.

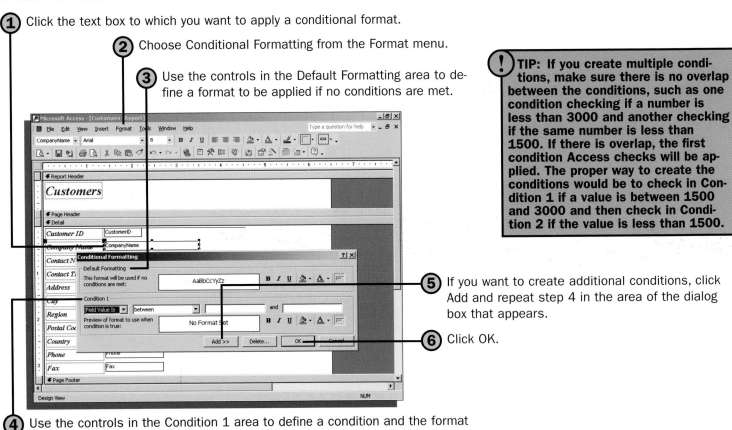

5 If you want to create additional conditions, click Add and repeat step 4 in the area of the dialog box that appears.

6 Click OK.

4 Use the controls in the Condition 1 area to define a condition and the format to be applied if the contents of the text box meet the condition.

Changing the Source of an Image

If you work with one organization for a while, you'll probably need to change the images on some of your forms and reports. Whether the change is to update the photograph of a product or to change from an old department logo to a new one, you can make the change quickly by identifying the new image in the control's Picture property. The advantage of making the change in the Properties box is that you save time by not deleting and replacing the previous image. Another consideration is that the image is placed in the same control, meaning you won't have to resize the image.

Define a New Image Source

1 Open a form or report in Design view.

2 Click the image for which you want to assign a new source.

3 Click the Properties button.

6 Click the Build button.

7 Navigate to the directory with the new image.

8 Double-click the image name.

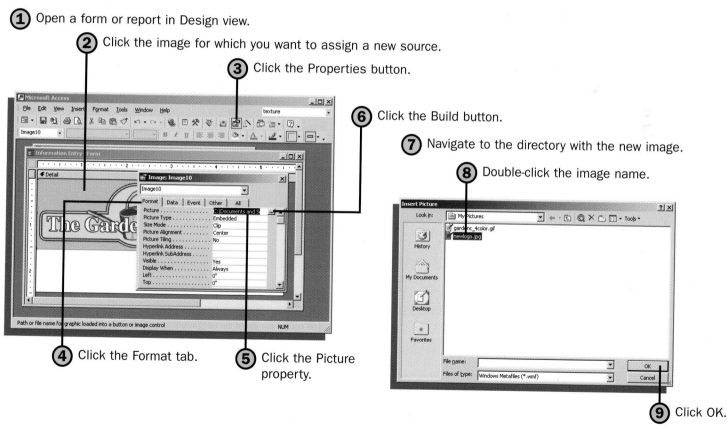

4 Click the Format tab.

5 Click the Picture property.

9 Click OK.

Setting Image Alignment and Backing Color

When you add an image to a form or report, you're actually creating a control and designating the image as the contents of that control. Because the image is contained within a control, you can use the edges of the control as a frame through which you and your colleagues view the image. As an example, suppose you have a large image illustrating a process, but the two critical areas you need to show on a form are in opposite corners of the image. By setting the image's alignment within the control, you can align the image so any corner is displayed, meaning you can display the sections of the image you need to show without manipulating the image itself. If there is space between the edge of the image and the control's border, you can fill the rest of the control with a background color to provide a frame around the image.

Set a Backing Color

SEE ALSO: For more information about formatting the borders of a control, see "Adding Lines, Shapes, and Borders" on page 127.

(1) Open a form or report in Design view.

(2) Click the image you want to format.

(4) Click the Format tab.

(3) Click the Properties button.

(5) Click the Back Style box.

(6) Click the down arrow.

(7) Click Normal.

(8) Click the Back Color box.

(9) Click the Build button.

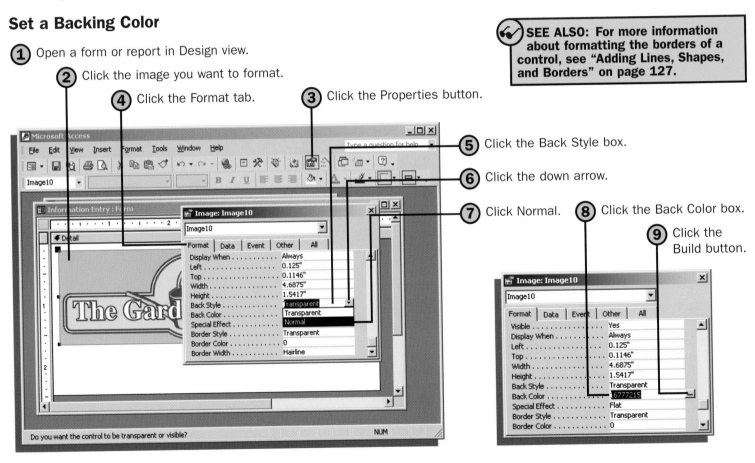

Change a Picture's Alignment

10 Click the color for the background of the control containing your image.

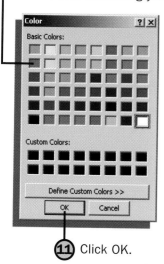

11 Click OK.

12 Click the Close box.

1 Click the image you want to format.

3 Click the Format tab.   **2** Click the Properties button.

7 Click the Close box.

6 Click the alignment you want to assign to your image.

5 Click the down arrow.

4 Click the Picture Alignment box.

> **!** **TIP: If you want to see the Detail section of the form or any objects behind the image, change the Back Style property's value to Transparent.**

Tiling a Picture

When you add an image to a form or report, you usually want the image to appear in one place. Some images are meant to be repeated, however. For example, you could create a small, square graphic with a repeating pattern, or *texture*, you'd like to appear as the background on your form or report. When you repeat an image, you use instances of the image like tiles in a mosaic—the images are placed side-by-side and cover the entire background of your form or report.

Repeat a Picture on a Form or Report

! **TIP:** You can find a number of textures in this directory: \Program Files\Microsoft Office\Office 10\Bitmaps\Styles. You can also buy textures in most software stores or create your own with a graphics program. The keys to creating a great texture are to make sure you can't see the edges of the individual graphics and to keep the texture file as small as possible.

(1) Open a form or report in Design view.

(2) Click the image you want to repeat on your form or report.

(3) Click the Properties button.

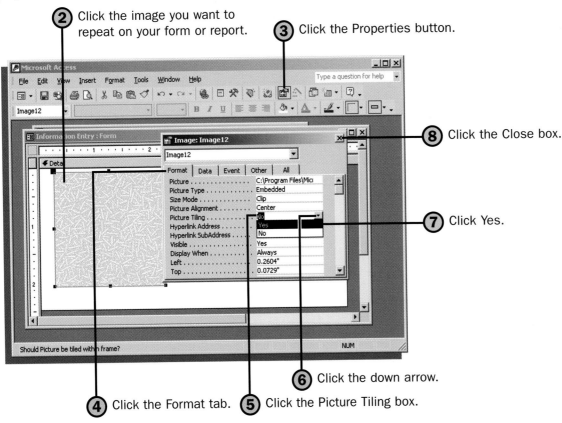

(8) Click the Close box.

(7) Click Yes.

(6) Click the down arrow.

(4) Click the Format tab. **(5)** Click the Picture Tiling box.

Controlling When an Image Appears

Corporate identification is important, whether you have created a report for your own use or for dissemination to the public. One way you can use objects such as text boxes and form and report graphics to identify the source of a document is to hide the graphic or text until a form or report is printed. The graphic could be a subtle pattern in one corner of the screen or the word *Proprietary* appearing in the center of the page, but either type of watermark would serve to identify the source and importance of the printout.

> **TIP:** To have an image or text box appear on the screen but not when the form or report is printed, set the Display When property to Screen Only.

Add a Watermark to a Form or Report

(1) Open a form or report in Design view.

(2) Click the image you want to use as your watermark.

(3) Click the Properties button.

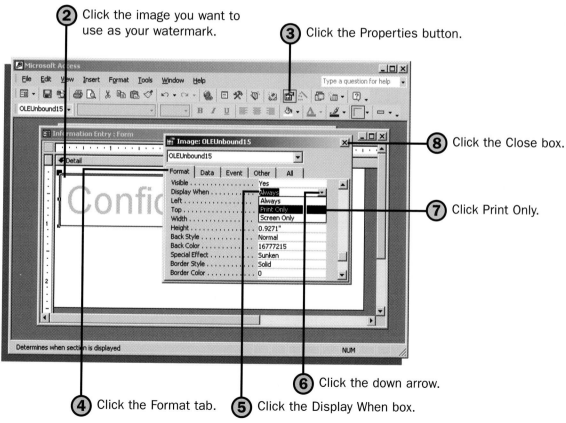

(8) Click the Close box.

(7) Click Print Only.

(6) Click the down arrow.

(4) Click the Format tab.

(5) Click the Display When box.

Setting Image Height and Width

When you design a form or report, you'll often have the freedom to move things around and make images as large or small as you need to. There will be times, however, when space on the page is at a premium and you need to define a specific space in which an image will appear. You can set the height and width of the control that will hold the image by setting its Height and Width properties in the Properties box.

You can also control how an image will react when its control is resized. If you want, you can have the image stretch to match the new frame size, remain the same size (and possibly be cropped), or resize the image to fit within the control while retaining the original image's height and width ratio.

Set a Precise Image Height and Width

(1) Open a form or report in Design view.

(2) Click the image you want to format.

(3) Click the Properties button.

> **TIP:** If you add an image to a form or report and want to ensure all other images you add to other database objects are the same size, you should write down the values in the Height and Width property boxes.

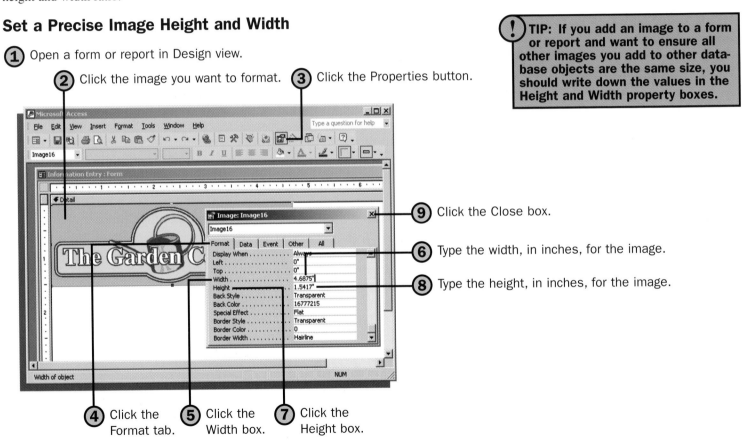

(9) Click the Close box.

(6) Type the width, in inches, for the image.

(8) Type the height, in inches, for the image.

(4) Click the Format tab.

(5) Click the Width box.

(7) Click the Height box.

Set an Image's Resizing Property

(1) Open a form or report in Design view.

(2) Click the image you want to format.

(3) Click the Properties button.

(✓) SEE ALSO: For information about changing how an image is aligned within a control, see "Setting Image Alignment and Backing Color" on page 134.

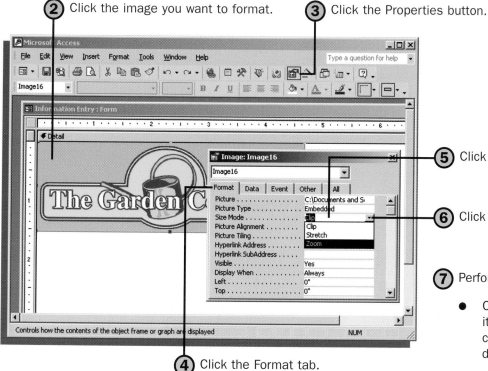

(5) Click the Size Mode box.

(6) Click the down arrow.

(7) Perform any of the following steps:

- Click Clip to display the image at its actual size. The image may be cropped at the bottom right if it doesn't fit in the control.

- Click Stretch to make the image fill the control. The image may be distorted.

- Click Zoom to display the entire image without changing its proportions. There may be blank space in the control.

(4) Click the Format tab.

Adding Clip Art to Forms and Reports

If you want to include a form in a presentation you give to your colleagues or in a report you make available on your company's Web site, you can add images from the Clip Art collection that comes with Office to accent your worksheet. You can manage your clip art with the Microsoft Clip Gallery or find additional images by searching for clip art on the Web.

Add Clip Art to a Form or Report

(1) Open a form or report in Design view, and choose Object from the Insert menu.

(2) Click Microsoft Clip Gallery. (3) Click OK.

(4) Click the Category from which you want to select the image.

(5) Click the clip you want to insert.

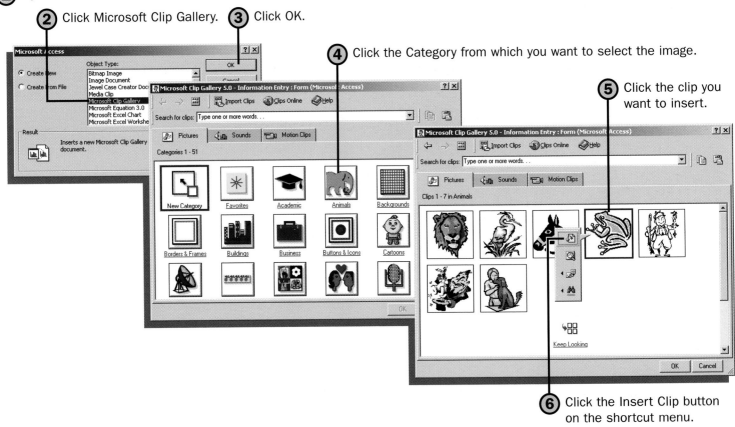

(6) Click the Insert Clip button on the shortcut menu.

Copy Clip Art from the Web

(1) Open a form or report in Design view, and choose Object from the Insert menu.

(2) Click Microsoft Clip Gallery. **(3)** Click OK.

(4) Click Clips Online.

!**TIP: To display a full-size preview of a clip art image, click the image.**

(5) Click OK to clear the message box that appears.

(6) When the Web page opens, click the category you want to browse.

(7) Select the check box next to any clip you want to download.

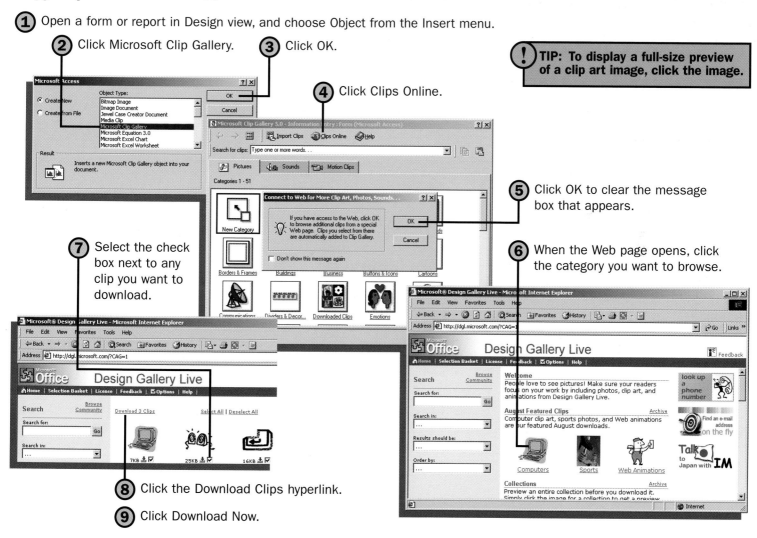

(8) Click the Download Clips hyperlink.

(9) Click Download Now.

Search for Clip Art on the Web

(1) Open a form or report in Design view, and choose Object from the Insert menu.

(2) Click Microsoft Clip Gallery.

(3) Click OK.

(4) Click Clips Online.

Microsoft Access

Object Type:
- Bitmap Image
- Image Document
- Jewel Case Creator Document
- Media Clip
- Microsoft Clip Gallery
- Microsoft Equation 3.0
- Microsoft Excel Chart
- Microsoft Excel Worksheet

○ Create New
○ Create from File

OK
Cancel
☐ Display as Icon

Result: Inserts a new Microsoft Clip Gallery object into your document.

Microsoft Clip Gallery 5.0 - Information Entry Form (Microsoft Access)

Import Clips   Clips Online   Help

Search for clips: Type one or more words...

Pictures | Sounds | Motion Clips

Categories 1 - 51

Connect to Web for More Clip Art, Photos, Sounds...

If you have access to the Web, click OK to browse additional clips from a special Web page. Clips you select from there are automatically added to Clip Gallery.

OK
Cancel

☐ Don't show this message again

New Category
Borders & Frames | Buildings | Business | Buttons & Icons | Cartoons
Communications | Dividers & Decor... | Downloaded Clips | Emotions | Entertainment

OK   Cancel

(5) Click OK to clear the message box that appears.

(6) Type a word that might appear in the description of the item you want to add.

Search   Browse Community

Search for:
globe   Go

Search in:
...

Results should be:
...

Order by:
...

(7) Click the Search In down arrow, and choose a location to search.

(8) Click the Results Should Be down arrow, and choose the type of item you want to find.

(9) Click Go.

> ✋ **CAUTION:** While you can use the images in the Microsoft Clip Gallery in your presentations, you should be absolutely sure you have the necessary rights to use images you draw from other sources.

Interacting with Other Programs

Microsoft Access is a powerful program, but it doesn't try to do everything. Other programs in the Microsoft Office XP suite have complementary strengths: Microsoft Word is great for creating text documents, Microsoft Excel is ideal for recording and analyzing financial information, and Microsoft PowerPoint lets you convert your thoughts into attractive presentations you can print out or project onto a screen for audiences in the hundreds.

Access also gives you a lot of versatility in interacting with other companies or individuals who might not keep their databases in Access. You can easily export your Access table data and query results into many other file formats or bring in data from the same programs.

In this chapter, you'll learn how to:

- Embed and link to existing objects.

- Create, modify, and move objects.

- Include Excel charts and worksheets in Access documents.

- Create your own charts from Access table and query data.

- Move data between Access and other programs.

Introducing Linking and Embedding

Access works wonderfully as a stand-alone program, but it really shines when you use it in combination with other programs. One way to use Access in conjunction with other programs is to include files created in other programs, such as graphics, text documents created in Word, PowerPoint presentations, or Excel charts and worksheets, in your forms and reports. You can add these objects to your database through *linking* and *embedding*.

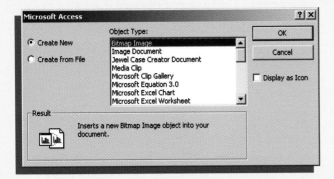

Linking and embedding are done through the same dialog box, but there are several important things you need to keep in mind when you're deciding whether to link to an object or to embed it in a form or a report. As the name implies, embedding an object in a form or report stores a copy of the object with the database. For example, if you wanted to add a company logo to an invoice generated from table data, you could identify the graphic and indicate you wanted to embed it in the database. The advantage of embedding an object in a database is that you never have to worry about the graphic, chart, or spreadsheet not being available because the person pulling up the form or report copied the database to a computer

without the embedded file. If you create databases with embedded files, you can travel anywhere, secure in the knowledge that the files will be there.

The downside to embedding objects in databases is that the embedded files can be quite large and increase the size of the database file significantly. While a single, low-resolution logo meant to be viewed on a computer monitor probably won't have much of an impact on your file size, the same image rendered at a resolution suitable for printing might double the size of the database. If you embed more than one image, or more than one copy of the same image, you might make your database unworkably large.

When you want to include more than one image or external file in an Access database, the best choice may be to create a link to the files in the form or report. For example, rather than embed many copies of a high-resolution logo in your reports, you could save the file on your computer and use the linking and embedding dialog box to identify the file's location on your computer. Access would use the reference to find the file and display it as part of a database object. The database would be no larger than it was originally, and you wouldn't need to have multiple copies of the same document if you link to it more than once. So, the advantage of linking is that you save disk space, but the disadvantage is that moving from computer to computer can be difficult unless you take the non-Access files with you when you travel. In general, you should embed an object in an Access database if you only use the object once and you have room to store the database (with the included object) when you travel. In other cases, such as when you use the same file multiple times in the same database, you should strongly consider linking to the file and not embedding it.

Inserting a New Object

Access tables and queries hold a lot of data, but you can augment your Access data with information in files created with other programs. For example, you might have created a Word document with important background information or a PowerPoint presentation that puts your data into context for your colleagues. You can include those files in your Access forms and reports by linking or embedding the files as *objects*.

Embed an Existing Object

① Open the form or report in Design view.

② Choose Object from the Insert menu.

⑤ Browse for the file you want to embed, and double-click it.

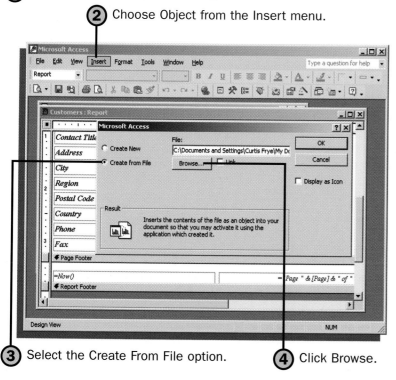

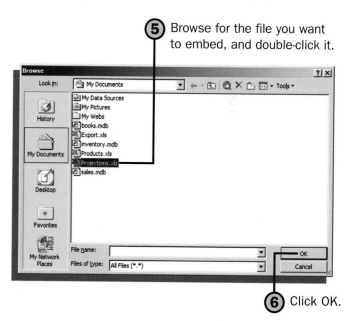

⑥ Click OK.

③ Select the Create From File option.

④ Click Browse.

Link to an Existing Object

① Open the form or report in Design view.

② Choose Object from the Insert menu.

③ Select the Create From File option.

TIP: If you want to link or embed an object but don't want it to take up much space on the form or report, select the Display As Icon check box to display the file's Windows icon instead of the object itself.

④ Select the Link check box.

⑤ Click Browse.

⑥ Browse for the file you want to include, and double-click it.

⑦ Click OK.

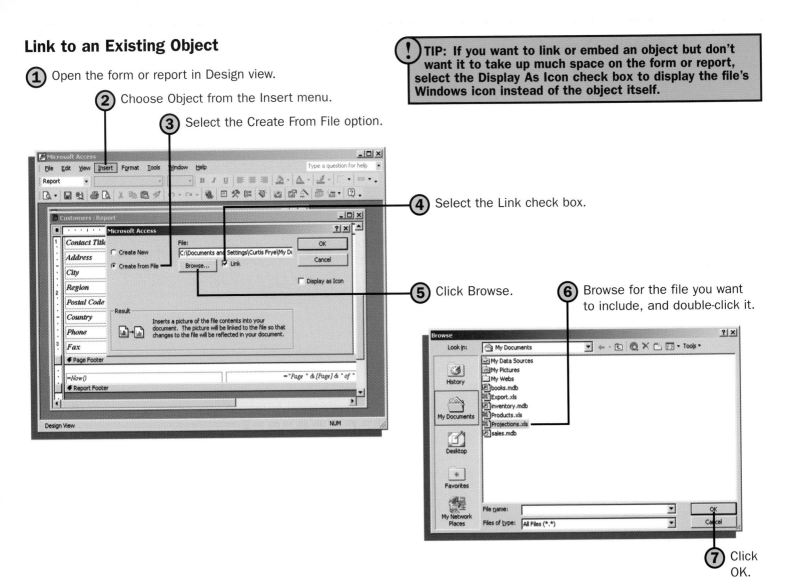

Manipulating Objects

Once you've added an object to a form or a report, you can work with it in the same way you would work with form or report controls. For example, if you wanted to display the same image at the top and bottom of a report, you could do so by adding the image to the report, copying it, and then pasting it at the bottom of the report.

Copy an Object

① Click the object you want to copy.

② Click the Copy button.

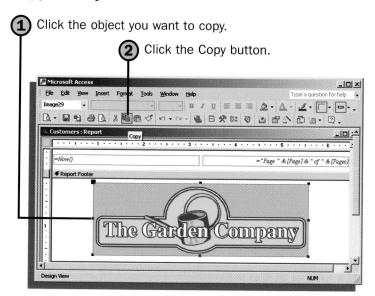

Paste an Object

① Open a form or report in Design view.

② Click in the form or report section where you want to paste the object.

③ Click the Paste button.

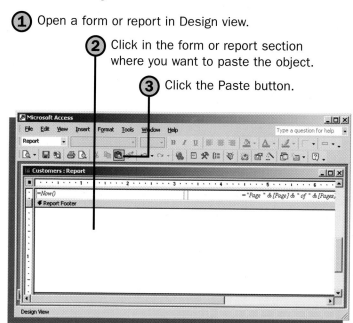

Move an Object

① Click the object you want to move.

② Drag the object to the new location on the form or report.

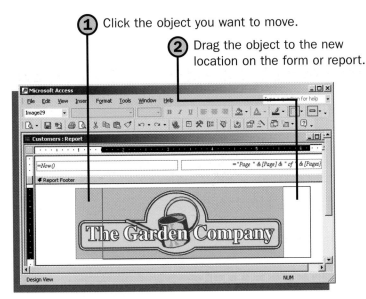

Resize an Object

① Click the object you want to resize.

② Drag one of the handles at the edge of the object to resize the object.

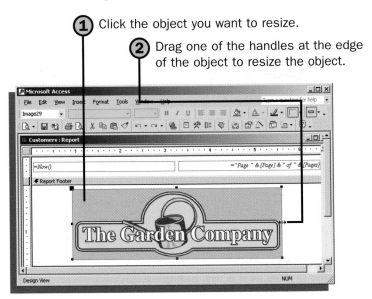

 SEE ALSO: For more information about arranging your objects on a form or a report, see "Setting Control Appearance" on page 122.

Inserting Excel Charts and Worksheets

Access is designed to let you store, manipulate, and ask questions of large amounts of data. Excel offers a wide range of data analysis and presentation tools you can use to extend the analysis you perform in Access. Including an Excel chart or worksheet in an Access form or report lets you explore alternative scenarios, use past data to project future patterns, or summarize your data in ways not available in Access summary queries.

Add an Excel Chart

① Open a form or report in Design view.

② Choose Object from the Insert menu.

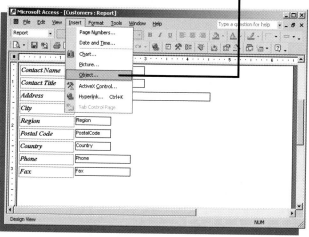

③ If necessary, select the Create New option.

④ Click Microsoft Excel Chart.

⑤ Click OK.

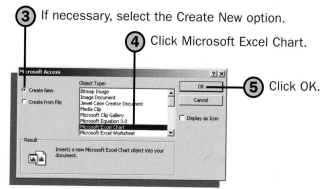

Add an Excel Worksheet

① Open a form or report in Design view.

② Choose Object from the Insert menu.

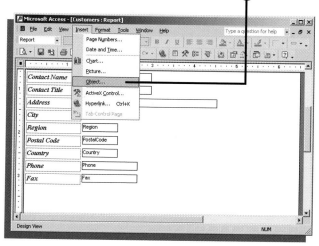

③ If necessary, select the Create New option.

④ Click Microsoft Excel Worksheet.

⑤ Click OK.

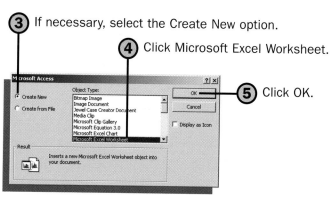

Creating a Chart

Access tables store lots of raw data—contact names, sales figures, prices, salaries, and so on. Raw numbers are great for calculations but aren't ideal when you need to describe the data to another human being. Charts and graphs, which summarize data visually, are very effective at communicating data values and trends, whether for your own use or for inclusion in a business report.

Build a New Chart

(1) Open a form or report in Design view, and choose Chart from the Insert menu.

(2) Drag in the body of the form or report to define the area for the chart.

(3) If necessary, select the Both option to display all available tables and queries.

(4) Click the table or query to provide the data for your chart, and click Next.

(5) Click a field to add to the chart, click Add to add it to the chart, and click Next.

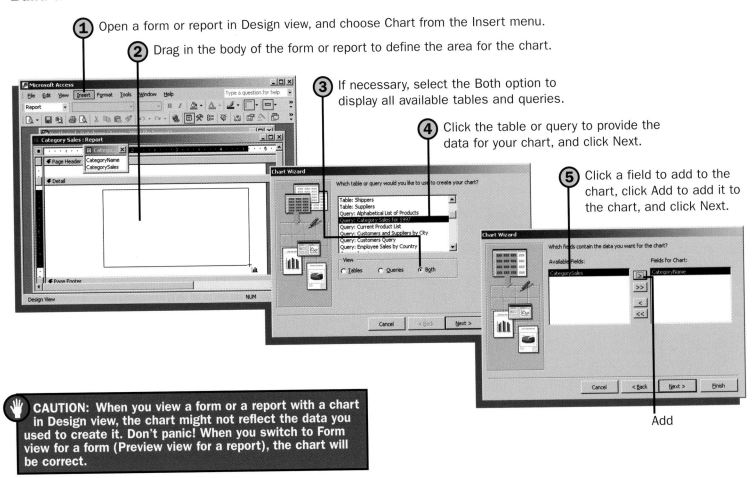

Add

CAUTION: When you view a form or a report with a chart in Design view, the chart might not reflect the data you used to create it. Don't panic! When you switch to Form view for a form (Preview view for a report), the chart will be correct.

! TIP: You can see what your chart will look like by clicking the Preview Chart button at the upper left of the wizard page.

6 Click the type of chart you want to create, and click Next.

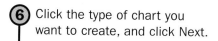

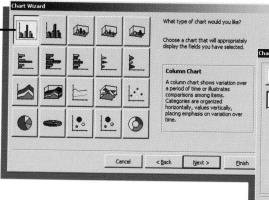

7 Use the controls on this wizard screen to determine the layout of your chart, and click Next.

8 To control how the chart varies based on the records shown in the form or report, click the first Report Fields down arrow, and click either of the following:

- <No Field> to have the chart remain constant.

- The field on which you want the chart to vary.

9 Click the corresponding Chart Fields down arrow, repeat your selection, and click Next.

10 Type a name for the report, and click Finish.

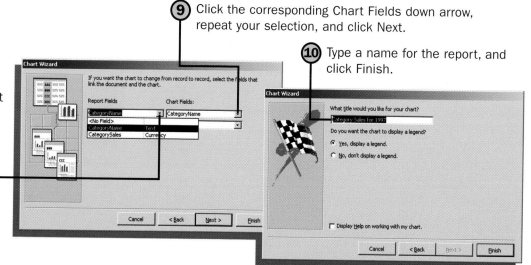

Bringing In Data from Other Programs

Access is great at storing your data, but you won't always have the data you want to summarize or query in an Access table. Fortunately, Access makes it easy to bring in data from many other popular programs. Once the data is in Access, you can combine it with your existing tables to build more comprehensive queries, forms, and reports. The steps you'll go through in the Import Data Wizard vary depending on the program used to create the data you're bringing in, but you'll find plenty of explanations to help you on your way.

> ✋ **CAUTION: Unless you are certain the data you're importing has a primary key field, you should have the wizard create a new primary key field. Even if you add the field unnecessarily, you can always delete it later.**

Import Data

① Point to Get External Data on the File menu, and then click Import.

④ Double-click the file containing the data you want to import.

⑤ Follow the instructions in the wizard to ensure the data will be read in properly.

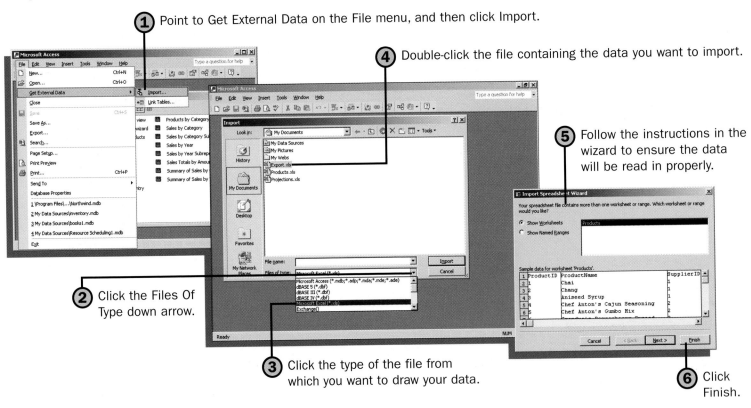

② Click the Files Of Type down arrow.

③ Click the type of the file from which you want to draw your data.

⑥ Click Finish.

Sending Data to Other Programs

Just as you can bring in data from other programs, you can save your Access tables and queries as files in the formats of other database and spreadsheet programs. The ability to save your data in a variety of formats makes it easy to exchange data with suppliers who use a different database program or traveling colleagues who may not have Access installed on their laptops. It's also easier to transfer financial data to Excel for further analysis using that program's specialized tools.

Export Data

TRY THIS: Open the Northwind sample database, and click Tables on the Objects bar. Click the Products table, and then choose Export from the File menu. Type Products **in the File Name box, click the Save As Type down arrow, click Microsoft Excel 97-2002 (*.xls), and then click Export. The Products table is now saved as an Excel worksheet.**

(1) Click the database object you want to export.

(2) Choose Export from the File menu.

(3) Click the Save As Type down arrow.

(4) Click the file format to which you want to export your data.

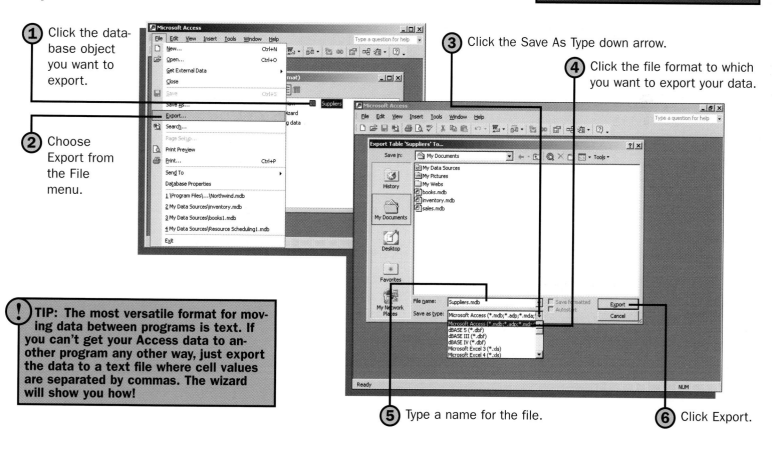

TIP: The most versatile format for moving data between programs is text. If you can't get your Access data to another program any other way, just export the data to a text file where cell values are separated by commas. The wizard will show you how!

(5) Type a name for the file.

(6) Click Export.

12 Sharing Database Data on the Web

One hallmark of Microsoft Access is that you can save your tables, queries, and other database objects as files that can be displayed and interacted with on the World Wide Web. Access 2002 extends those capabilities, adding entirely new functions and making existing capabilities easier to use.

A new technology that makes its debut in Access 2002 is the Extensible Markup Language (XML). XML is a content markup language, meaning that an XML file has information about the data contained within it (as compared to the Hypertext Markup Language, or HTML, which tells a Web browser how to display a file's contents).

In this chapter, you'll learn how to:

- Create hyperlinks to files and Web pages.

- Save a database object as a Web page.

- Create data access pages.

- Format and manipulate data in data access pages.

- Import and export database objects using XML.

Integrating Access and the Internet

The Internet is an important business tool. Whether you're sending e-mail to collaborators ten time zones away or putting your company's catalog on a Web site so that your customers can get information about your products at their convenience, you can use the Internet to streamline your business processes or find important information.

Access gives you lots of tools to use the Internet, and particularly the Web, to your advantage. Perhaps the most basic and useful technique is to save a database object as an HTML file. HTML is the language Web site creators use to tell a Web browser how to display the data it encounters in files on the Web. To impart that display information, designers enclose the text to be displayed in *tags*. One simple tag pair, <B>...</B>, tells Web browsers to display the text between the tags in bold font. So, <B>Grand Total</B> would be displayed as **Grand Total**. There are literally hundreds of different tags, but you don't need to worry about knowing any of them. When you save your database object as an HTML file, Access does all the work for you.

Use the Web Toolbar

If you want to visit Web sites while you're using Access, you can display the Web toolbar and use its controls to go to your favorite sites, refresh the Web page you're visiting to see if it has changed, or search the Web for information. The graphic below shows the Web toolbar and points out the controls available to you. The graphic on the left shows how an Access table, saved as an HTML file, appears in a Web browser.

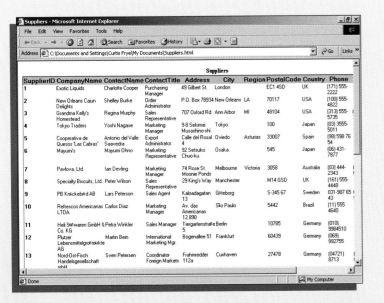

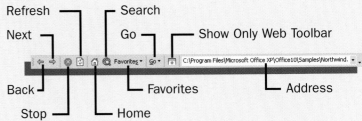

Working with Hyperlinks

A fundamental characteristic of the World Wide Web is the ability to create connections—called *hyperlinks*—between related documents. By creating hyperlinks to helpful files on the Web, or even to objects in the current Access database, you can provide useful information to anyone viewing the Web page. Those documents may in turn have links that lead you away from the main document. You can easily return to the database page quickly using the Web toolbar's Back button or, if a hyperlink leads to a Web page viewed in a Web browser, you can simply switch back to the Access window. Hyperlinks to Web pages start with *http://*, but a hyperlink to a file in the same directory as the database would consist of just the file's name.

Add a Hyperlink Field to a Table

1 Click Tables on the Objects bar.

3 Click Design. **2** Click a table.

4 Type a name for the new field, and press the Tab key.

5 Click the down arrow.

6 Click Hyperlink.

7 Press the Tab key, and type a comment describing the field.

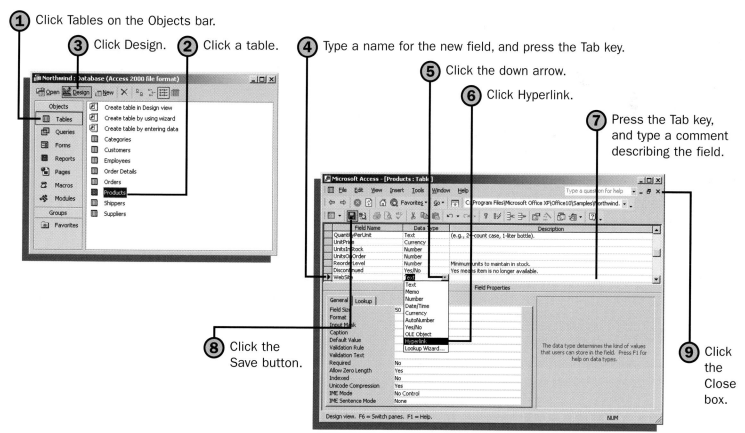

8 Click the Save button.

9 Click the Close box.

Create a Hyperlink to an Existing Web Page or File

1 Open the form or report in Design view.

2 Click the Insert Hyperlink button.

3 If necessary, click Existing File Or Web Page.

4 Use the controls in the dialog box to identify the file to which you want to link.

5 Type the text you want to appear in the form or report.

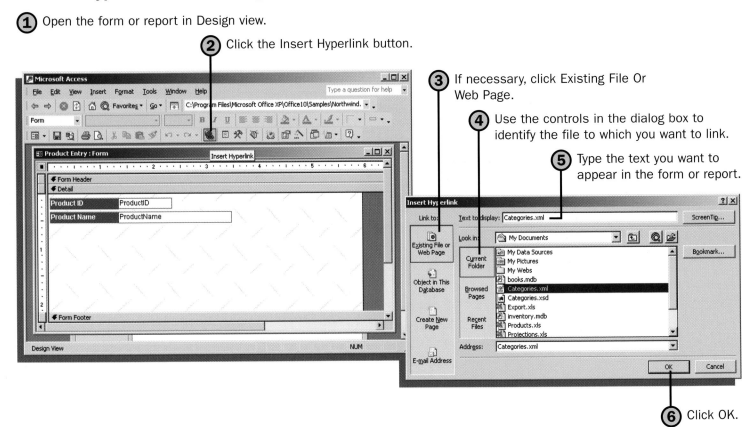

6 Click OK.

Create a Hyperlink to an Existing Database Object

① Open the form or report in Design view.

② Click the Insert Hyperlink button.

③ If necessary, click Object In This Database.

④ Click the plus sign next to the type of object to which you want to link.

⑤ Click the object to which you want to link.

⑥ Type the text to be displayed in the form or report.

⑦ Click OK.

! TIP: If you want to create a hyperlink that is activated when an object or some text is clicked, select the object or text and then click the Insert Hyperlink button.

Saving Database Objects as Web Pages

One of the easiest ways to communicate data to traveling colleagues is to make that data available on a Web page. Writing the data to a Web page means you don't have to send the entire database file to the traveler. In fact, your colleague doesn't even need Access on his or her machine! Saving database objects as Web pages is also a great way to make data available over a corporate network (an *intranet*). So long as your company's network supports Web connections, you can make your data available to any authorized user.

Save an Object as a Web Page

(1) Click the object you want to save as a Web page.

(2) Choose Export from the File menu.

(3) Click the Save As Type down arrow.

(4) Click HTML Documents (*.html; *.htm).

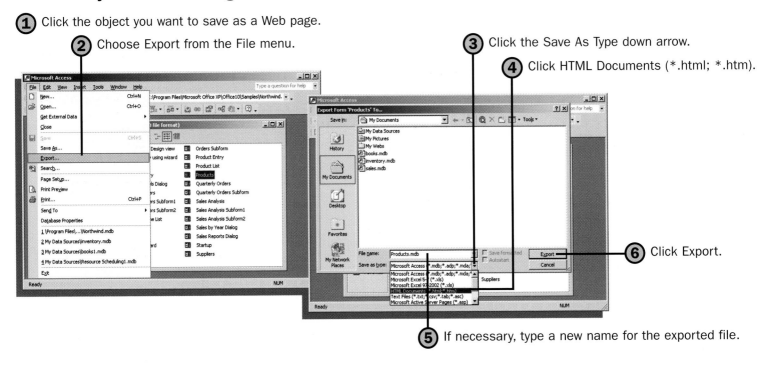

(6) Click Export.

(5) If necessary, type a new name for the exported file.

Creating a Data Access Page

Data access pages, sometimes just called *pages*, are a combination report and Web document. Reports let you present your table and query data using the grouping method of your choice, while Web pages let you make your tables and query data available to users who can reach your company's network. Data access pages let you do both, meaning you can make your data available over the Web and organize it any way you want. As an added bonus, anyone viewing a data access page can show or hide entire categories of data, letting them focus on the data they need to make an important business decision.

Create a Data Access Page Using the Page Wizard

1 Click Pages on the Objects bar.

2 Double-click Create Access Page By Using Wizard.

4 Use the Add, Add All, Remove, or Remove All buttons to select fields for the Selected Fields list.

5 Click Next.

3 Click the Tables/Queries down arrow, and click the table or query to provide the records for the data access page.

6 Click any fields by which you want to group the records in the data access page.

7 Click the Add button.

13 Type a name for the data access page.

14 Click Finish.

8 Click Next.

9 Click the first field's down arrow.

11 If desired, click the Ascending button to change the sort order to Descending.

10 Click the name of the field by which you want to sort the records displayed in the data access page.

12 Click Next.

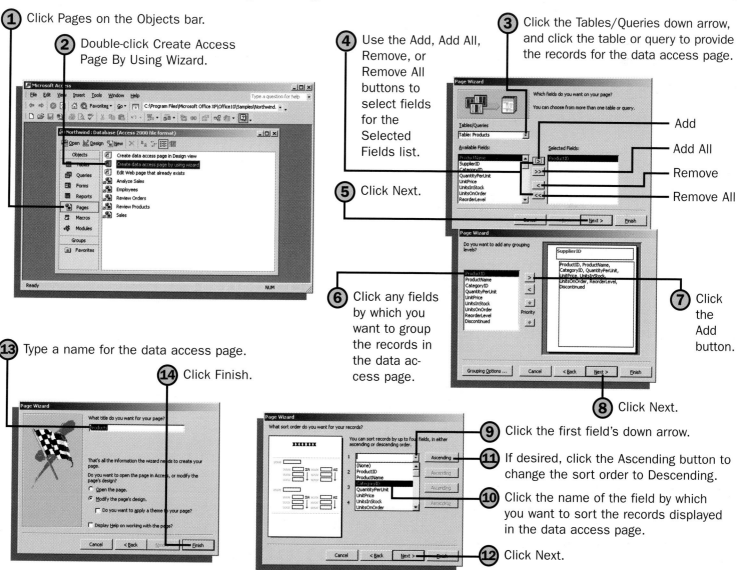

Add
Add All
Remove
Remove All

Arranging Data on a Data Access Page

Like forms and reports, you can change the appearance of your data access pages to present your data most effectively. For example, you can change the order in which the records appear on the page by adding grouping levels. When you add a grouping level to a data access page, all of the records in one group will appear before the records in the next group. For example, you could group a data access page created from the Northwind database's Customers table by country and show every customer from one country before moving to the next country.

Add a Grouping Level to a Data Access Page

① Open the data access page you want to edit in Design view.

② Click the field by which you want to group the contents of the data access page.

③ Click the Promote button.

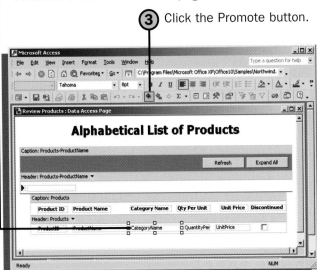

Remove a Grouping Level from a Data Access Page

① Open the data access page you want to edit in Design view.

② Click the field used to group the contents of the data access page.

③ Click the Demote button until the field appears in the body of the data access page.

Show Data in a Category

① Click Pages on the Objects bar.

② Click the page you want to view.

③ Click Open.

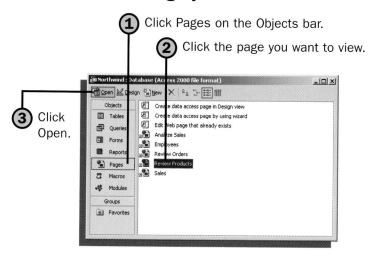

④ Click the right-pointing triangle to view the data in that category.

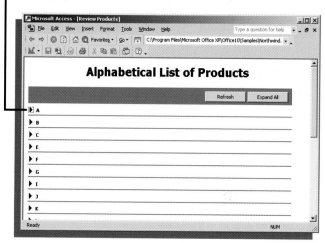

Hide Data in a Category

① Click Pages on the Objects bar.

② Click the page you want to view.

③ Click Open.

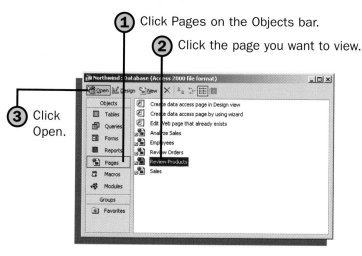

④ Click the down-pointing triangle to hide the data in that category.

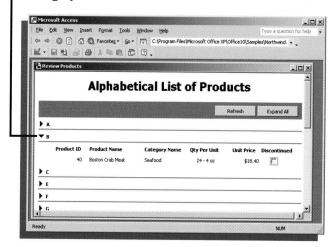

Viewing and Formatting a Data Access Page

When you create a data access page, you are actually creating a special kind of HTML file that acts as a gateway for the data behind it. You need Microsoft Internet Explorer 5 or later to view data access pages—when you open them, you can use the navigation tools at the bottom of a group to move between records in that group. You can also change the appearance of a data access page by applying a *theme*. Like an AutoFormat for a form or report, themes give you a selection of attractive, coordinated looks for your data access pages.

View a Data Access Page

1 Click the Windows Start button, point to Programs, and then click Internet Explorer.

2 Choose Open from the File menu.

3 Click Browse.

4 Browse for the file you want to open, and click it.

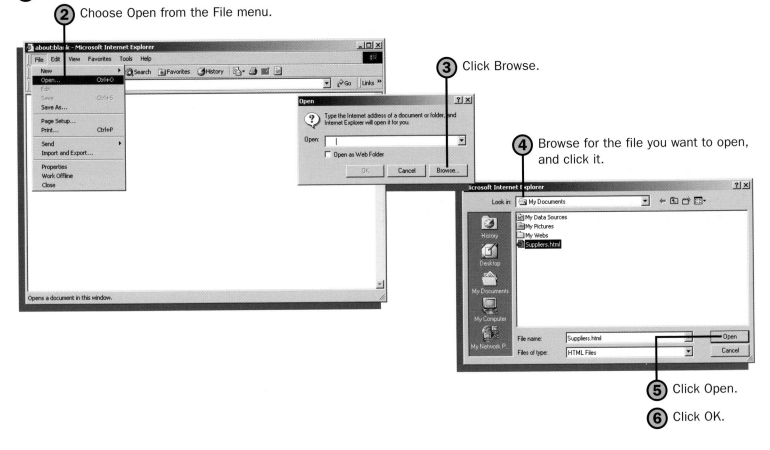

5 Click Open.

6 Click OK.

Style a Page with a Theme

(1) Open a data access page in Design view.

(2) Choose Theme from the Format menu.

! TIP: You can add and modify controls to a data access page just as you can with a form or report. For information about working with forms, reports, and data access pages in Design view, see "Setting Control Appearance" on page 122.

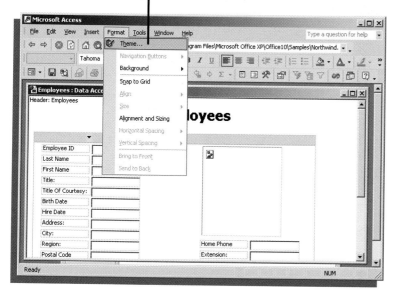

(3) Click the theme you want to apply to the data access page.

(4) Click OK.

! TIP: You can set a theme as the default design for your data access pages by opening a page in Design view, choosing Theme from the Format menu, clicking the theme to set as the default, clicking the Set Default button, and then clicking OK in the confirmation dialog box that appears.

Introducing XML

While HTML is great for describing how a Web page should be displayed in a browser, the language isn't designed to communicate anything about the contents of a document. For example, telling Internet Explorer to display an Access database table as an HTML table tells you nothing about the data shown on a Web page. When you save your table and query data to an XML document, however, Access annotates the data with tags describing which program generated the data, the name of the table, and the data that belongs in each table cell. With that information, Access, or another database program that understands XML data, can read in your tables and retain your original meaning.

Here's what the first record in the Northwind sample database's Suppliers table (shown in the graphic below) looks like in XML:

```
<SupplierID>1</SupplierID>
<CompanyName>Exotic Liquids</CompanyName>
<ContactName>Charlotte Cooper</ContactName>
<ContactTitle>Purchasing Manager</ContactTitle>
<Address>49 Gilbert St.</Address>
<City>London</City>
<PostalCode>EC1 4SD</PostalCode>
<Country>UK</Country>
<Phone>(171) 555-2222</Phone>
```

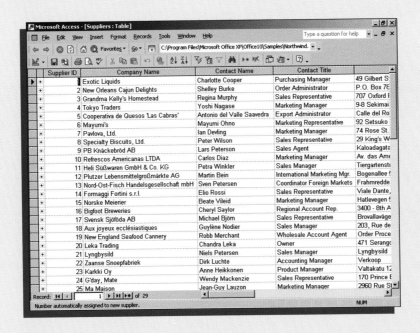

Using XML to Exchange Access Data

The goal of XML is to be a universal language, allowing data to move freely fro one application to another. This means that saving an Access table as an XML document allows any other database program to read the XML file, separate out the table column names and cell data, and use the annotations to recreate the table.

Save a Table as an XML Document

2 Choose Export from the File menu.

1 Click the database object you want to save as an XML document.

3 Click the Save As Type down arrow.

4 Click XML Documents (*.xml).

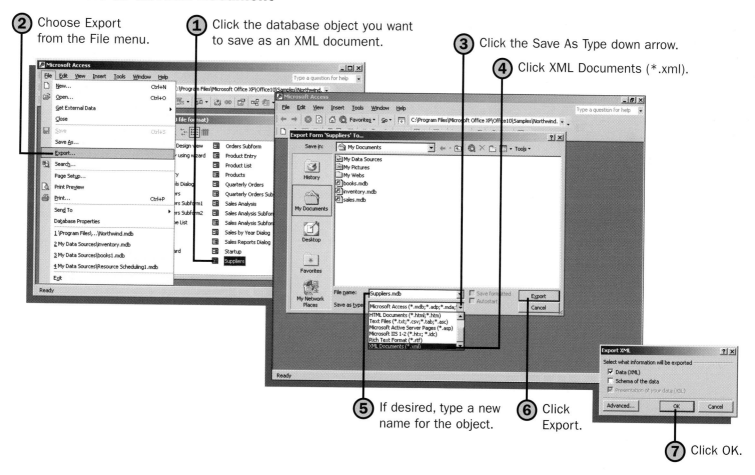

5 If desired, type a new name for the object.

6 Click Export.

7 Click OK.

Import XML Data

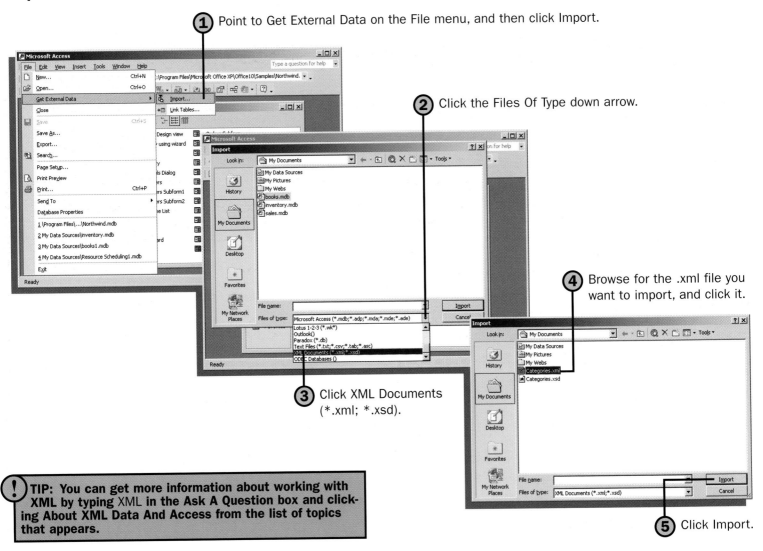

① Point to Get External Data on the File menu, and then click Import.

② Click the Files Of Type down arrow.

③ Click XML Documents (*.xml; *.xsd).

④ Browse for the .xml file you want to import, and click it.

⑤ Click Import.

> **TIP:** You can get more information about working with XML by typing XML in the Ask A Question box and clicking About XML Data And Access from the list of topics that appears.

13

Administering a Database

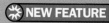

When working with sensitive data, you need to ensure that only authorized individuals are able to read the data. For example, if you manage a database containing your co-worker's salary information and performance reviews, you should do as much as you can to keep the database in good working order and to ensure that no one has access to that information unless they need it.

Access has a range of security and administration tools you can use to protect sensitive data while still allowing folks with a legitimate need to get at the data with as little hassle as possible. Those tools range from requiring your colleagues to enter passwords to use a database to the Documenter utility that prints out the vital statistics of every object in your database.

In this chapter, you'll learn how to:

● Create a workgroup information file.

● Set user guidelines with the User-Level Security Wizard.

● Encrypt a database.

● Compact and repair a database.

● Convert Access databases to other program versions.

● Create a switchboard.

● Document your database.

Introducing Database Security

At their heart, databases are programs to store important data. Whether you're protecting your friends' privacy by ensuring no one else opens your contacts database or preventing your colleagues from accidentally modifying or deleting important business data, database security is a critical part of using Access on computers connected to a network. In Access, though, security isn't necessarily an all-or-nothing choice. You can certainly set a single user account and password for a database and limit use of the database to those few folks who know the codes, but you also have a lot of flexibility in setting up individual accounts and tailoring that person's abilities, or *permissions*, to his or her needs.

Creating a Workgroup Information File

The first step in securing a database is to create a *workgroup information file*. A workgroup information file holds the security settings for one or more databases. The workgroup information file that comes with Access has no accounts or permissions set, so anyone can open any database and do whatever they want. If you want to change that, the first thing you need to do is set up a workgroup information file so that Access can track your security settings. To do that, you run the Workgroup Administrator and either create a new file (usually the best choice) or identify the existing file you want to use.

Turning on Database Security

After you've identified a workgroup information file, you turn on database security by setting a logon password for the database. Once you set the logon password, you can create individual accounts using the User-Level Security Wizard.

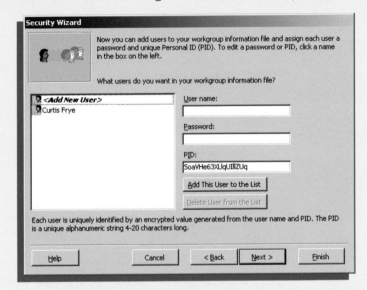

When you first run the wizard, you create accounts for you and your colleagues, assigning each individual a user name and a password. Each individual should enter his or her

> **! TIP: The User-Level Security Wizard may not have been installed when Access was added to your machine. To install the wizard, put your Microsoft Office CD in your computer's CD drive. When you insert the CD, Access will recognize the CD as the Office XP file source and identify it in the message box. Click Yes in the message box, and follow the instructions to install the wizard.**

own password if possible—as the Administrator, you don't need to know their passwords! Once you've established someone's account, you can assign him or her to a group or give him or her specific permissions. Also, if someone who needs to use the database leaves the company or moves to a project where he or she no longer has to use the data, you should delete the account immediately.

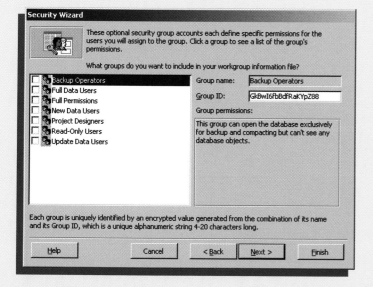

Choosing Passwords

Because they're so important to good security, in Access and elsewhere, a quick note about passwords is in order. The best passwords are random strings of characters, but random characters are hard to remember. One good method of creating hard-to-guess passwords is to combine elements of two words, mixing uppercase and lowercase letters, with a number in between to generate a character string that is at least eight characters long. For example, if you know something about horseback riding, you might have a password of *StiRrO3rt*, which could be read as "stirrups, three notches higher on the right." In any event, avoid passwords that are simple dictionary words in English or any other language, as they can be found easily by password-guessing programs available on the Internet. Substituting numbers for letters in dictionary words, as in *cOOl*, is no better because all substitutions are included in the password-guessing programs.

Encrypting Databases

Another technique you can use to prevent unauthorized users from getting at your data is to encrypt the database. When you create a database, the data and structural information used to create the database is stored as plain text, which can be read quickly and easily. The problem is that the same information can be read by opening the file in a word processor. So, even if you've set user accounts and passwords for your database, it's still possible to read the underlying data. To prevent unauthorized viewing, you can scramble the information used to create the database. Access can read the data without difficulty, but the database will run about 10 to 15 percent slower because of the additional processing required. It's important to remember that "encrypting" a database doesn't protect your data if you send it to the wrong person or someone copies the database. While no one can read the file with Word or another word processor, they will be able to with Access!

Creating a Workgroup Information File

The first step in securing a database is to create a workgroup information file. The workgroup information file holds information about the security settings for a database—which user accounts you've created, what security settings you've created for the database, and the password required to use the database. One nice thing about creating a workgroup information file is that you can use it for more than one database. If you want to use existing user accounts and groups for a second database, all you need to do is choose the workgroup information file with the desired settings.

> ✋ **CAUTION:** For the best security, create a new workgroup information file for each database. You should also change the name of the file so it isn't the same as the name of the database. That way, it's hard for the bad guys to find the file and modify it.

Create a Workgroup File

① Point to Security on the Tools menu, and then click Workgroup Administrator.

③ Type your name.

④ Type the name of your organization.

⑤ Type a string of up to twenty characters as a Workgroup ID.

⑥ Click OK.

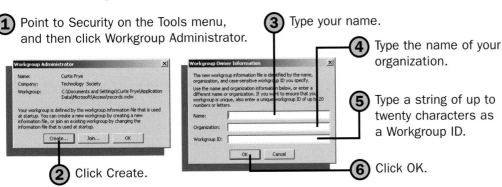

② Click Create.

⑦ Click OK to accept the directory Access selects for the file.

⑧ Click OK three times to confirm your information and create the workgroup.

Join an Existing Workgroup

① Point to Security on the Tools menu, and then click Workgroup Administrator.

③ Click Browse.

⑤ Click OK to close the Workgroup Information File dialog box.

④ Double-click the file.

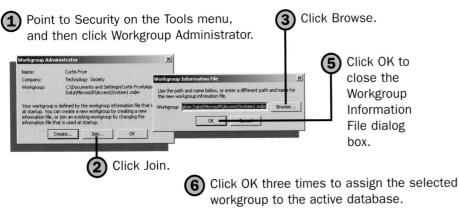

② Click Join.

⑥ Click OK three times to assign the selected workgroup to the active database.

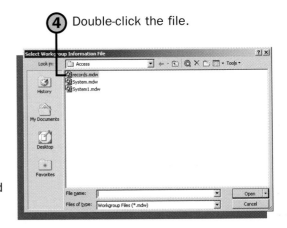

Requiring a Password to Open a Database

After you've joined a workgroup, you should require a password from anyone trying to open your database. To do that, you set a password for the Admin, or Administrator, account. Logging into a database using the Admin account means that you can do whatever you want to the database—change its layout, delete objects, or even delete everything and leave it empty. With that much power, it's a good idea to protect the Admin account.

SEE ALSO: For information about assigning permissions to individual users, see "Creating User Accounts" on page 174.

Assign an Admin Password

① Point to Security on the Tools menu, and then click User And Group Accounts.

② Click the Change Logon Password tab.

③ Type the new password.

TIP: Leave the Old Password field blank—you haven't assigned one yet!

User and Group Accounts ?| x|

Users | Groups | Change Logon Password |

User
Name: Admin ▾

New... | Delete | Clear Password

Group Membership
Available Groups: Member Of:
Admins | Admins
Users | Users

Add >>
<< Remove

Print Users and Groups

OK | Cancel | Apply

User and Group Accounts ?| x|

Users | Groups | Change Logon Password

User Name: Admin
Old Password:
New Password:
Verify:

④ Retype the new password to verify it.

OK | Cancel | Apply

⑤ Click OK.

CAUTION: Don't use your e-mail password for the database. That way, if you give someone the Admin password, you won't be giving them the password to your e-mail account as well!

Creating User Accounts

The best way to determine who can work with a database is to put the database on a computer with no network connection and lock the office door. That way, only people to whom you've given keys to the office can access the database. Access offers you other ways to determine who can use your database. You can use the User-Level Security Wizard to determine which tasks individual users can perform. If a user needs to read data from sales tables in the database but doesn't need to see the personal contact information of your customers, you can use the wizard's controls to limit the tables, queries, and reports that person can see. There's a lot going on, but the wizard has plenty of explanatory text to help you on your way.

Run the User-Level Security Wizard

① Point to Security on the Tools menu, and then click User-Level Security Wizard.

② If necessary, select the Create A New Workgroup Information File option, and click Next.

③ Type your name.

④ Type your company's name, and click Next.

⑤ If necessary, click the All Objects tab.

⑥ Click Select All, and click Next.

SEE ALSO: For information about activating user-level security, see "Requiring a Password to Open a Database" on page 173.

TRY THIS: To get more help on the User-Level Security Wizard, type user security in the Ask A Question box and then click the Secure An Access Database And Its Objects With User-Level Security topic.

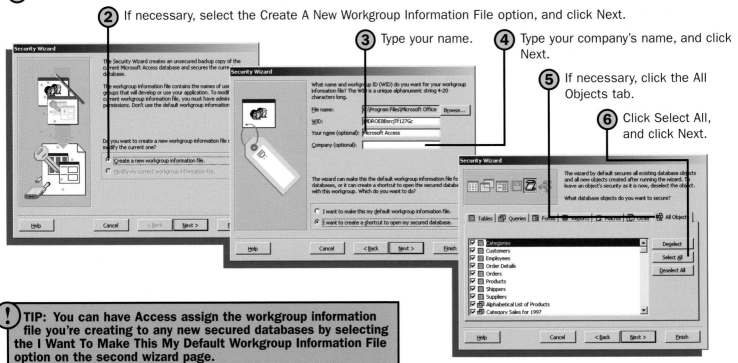

TIP: You can have Access assign the workgroup information file you're creating to any new secured databases by selecting the I Want To Make This My Default Workgroup Information File option on the second wizard page.

⑦ Select the check boxes of the groups you want to create, and click Next.

! TIP: You can find out which tasks members of a particular group can do by clicking the group's name and then reading the information in the Group Permissions area.

! TIP: To delete a user account, click the user's name and then click Delete User From The List.

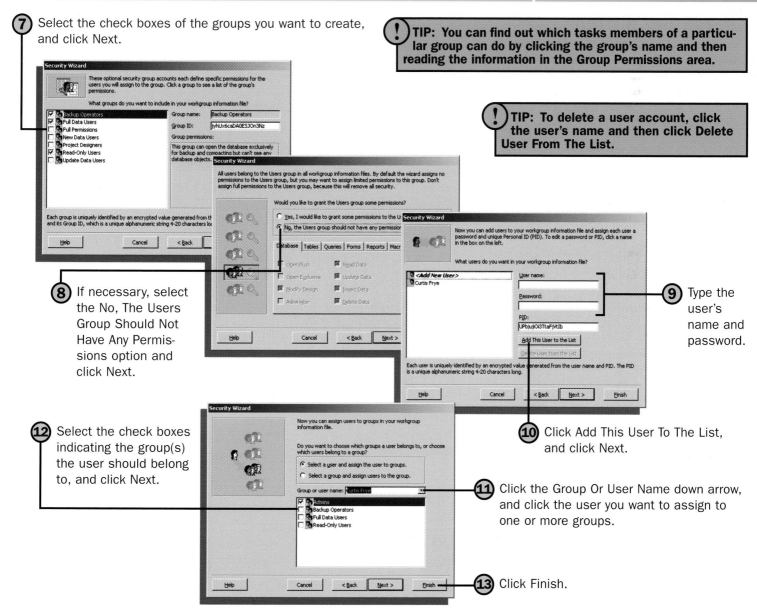

⑧ If necessary, select the No, The Users Group Should Not Have Any Permissions option and click Next.

⑨ Type the user's name and password.

⑩ Click Add This User To The List, and click Next.

⑪ Click the Group Or User Name down arrow, and click the user you want to assign to one or more groups.

⑫ Select the check boxes indicating the group(s) the user should belong to, and click Next.

⑬ Click Finish.

Encrypting a Database

One important thing to consider when you work with Access is that it's possible to view and edit the contents of an Access database using a word processor, such as Microsoft Word. You won't see the tables in the same easy-to-use layout you get when you open the database in Access, but all the data is there. In other words, storing your database on a computer without Access is no guarantee your data is safe from prying eyes. Fortunately, obscuring the contents of your database, or *encrypting* the database, is simple to do.

Encrypt a Database

(1) Point to Security on the Tools menu, and then click Encrypt/Decrypt Database.

(2) Type a name for the encrypted version of the database.

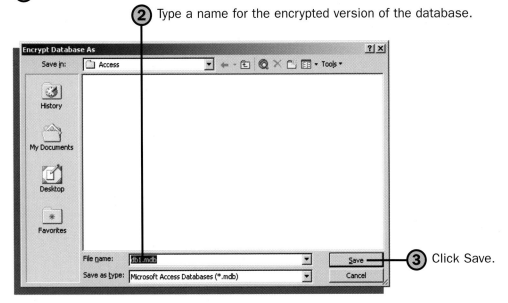

(3) Click Save.

Locking Database Records

Forms are versatile objects—you can use them to browse a database table or your query results, or to enter or modify table records. There might be some forms, however, that let your colleagues peek into tables where the records are too important to be modified. To prevent accidents in which important data gets deleted by well-meaning computer users, you can set a form's properties so the ability to add, modify, and delete records is turned off.

Lock Records in a Form

① Open a form in Design view.

② Double-click the form selector.

③ If necessary, click the Data tab.

④ Click Allow Edits.

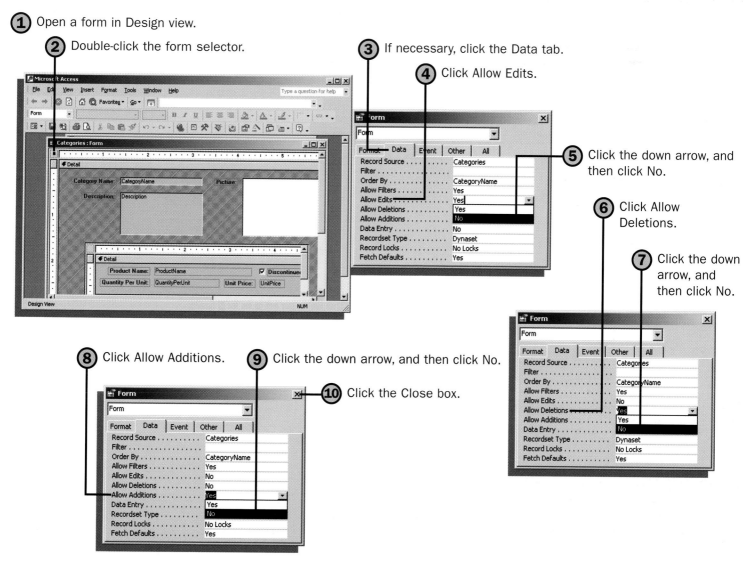

⑤ Click the down arrow, and then click No.

⑥ Click Allow Deletions.

⑦ Click the down arrow, and then click No.

⑧ Click Allow Additions.

⑨ Click the down arrow, and then click No.

⑩ Click the Close box.

Compacting and Repairing a Database

When you create and manipulate a database, you write and rewrite a lot of data. Whether you're adding new database records, editing existing records, or running queries to update the values in a table, there's a lot for Access to keep track of. To save space on your hard disk, and to ensure the database runs as quickly and efficiently as possible, you should compact your database every so often to make disk space available to other programs.

The other side of compacting and repairing a database is the repair operation. While data management errors are few and far between, it is possible that the battery might run out on your laptop, a co-worker could flip the wrong fuse, or lightning could strike nearby and cut off your power. If that happens, Access might not save the file correctly. The new Crash Recovery function could help, but you could also prevent problems by running the repair operation on a regular basis.

Compact a Database

① Point to Database Utilities on the Tools menu, and then click Compact And Repair Database.

> ⚠ **TIP: You can cancel the compact and repair sequence by pressing the Esc key.**

Repair a Database

① Start Microsoft Access without opening a database.

② Point to Database Utilities on the Tools menu, and then click Compact And Repair Database.

③ Double-click the database to repair.

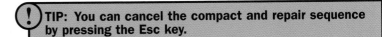

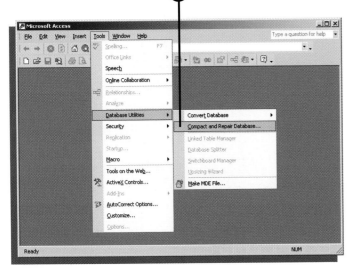

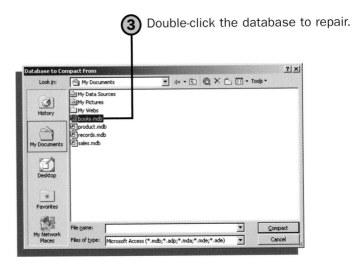

Converting Access Databases ⊕ NEW FEATURE

One benefit of working with Access is that you can take advantage of how much Access 2002 has in common with previous versions. In fact, if you don't change the program's settings, your files will be saved in the Access 2000 file format and you and your colleagues will be able to work with the files using Access 2000. The stability of the underlying database management system also means you can convert your Access 2000 and 2002 databases to the Access 97 file format, should you need to do so.

Convert an Access Database to Another Version

1 Point to Database Utilities on the Tools menu, point to Convert Database, and then click the target version.

- If necessary, click OK in any message boxes that appear, such as the box that lets you know any security settings you've created won't stay with the database after it is converted.

SEE ALSO: For information about sharing Access data with users of other programs, see "Sending Data to Other Programs" on page 153.

TIP: If you want to ensure that your database can only be opened with Access 2002, preventing the loss of any information or capabilities that would occur if the database were saved as an Access 2000 file, convert the file to Access 2002.

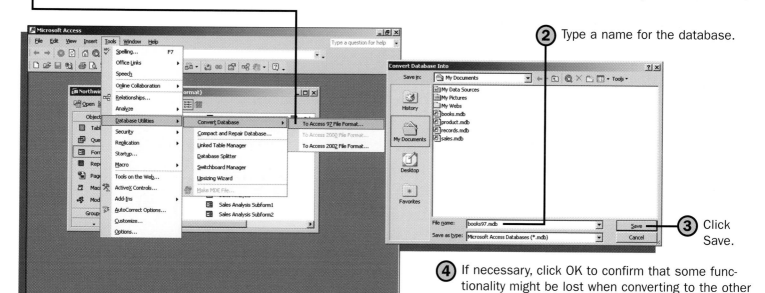

2 Type a name for the database.

3 Click Save.

4 If necessary, click OK to confirm that some functionality might be lost when converting to the other version of Access.

Creating a Switchboard

When you open the Northwind sample database, a navigation form appears to help you find common tasks and data sources. This form, called a *switchboard*, contains controls you can click to view product and order information, print a sales report, open the database window, or even exit Access. If you create a database using a database wizard, the wizard creates a switchboard form for you. If you create a database from scratch, or if you deleted the switchboard from a wizard-created database, you can build your own switchboard. In either case, you can edit the switchboard to add, delete, or modify the controls available to on the first or subsequent pages.

Create a Blank Switchboard

(1) Point to Database Utilities on the Tools menu, and then click Switchboard Manager.

(2) Click Yes to create a new switchboard.

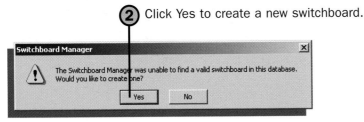

Add a Switchboard Page

(1) Point to Database Utilities on the Tools menu, and then click Switchboard Manager.

(2) Click New.

(3) Type a name for the new switchboard page.

(4) Click OK.

(5) Click Close in the Switchboard Manager dialog box.

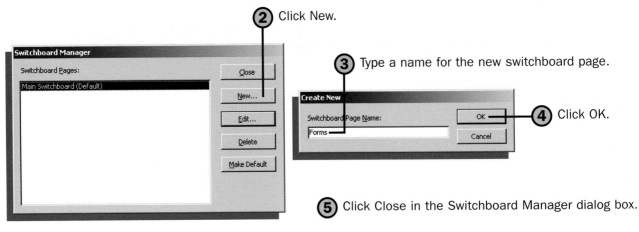

Add an Item to a Switchboard Page

① Point to Database Utilities on the Tools menu, and then click Switchboard Manager.

TIP: The name of the final list of available targets will change depending on the command you choose.

② Click the switchboard page to which you want to add an item.

③ Click Edit.

④ Click New.

⑤ Type the identifying text for the item.

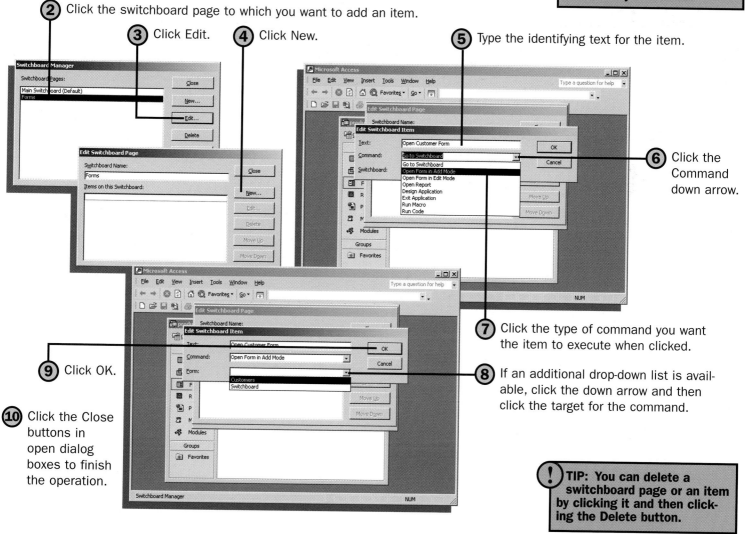

⑥ Click the Command down arrow.

⑦ Click the type of command you want the item to execute when clicked.

⑨ Click OK.

⑧ If an additional drop-down list is available, click the down arrow and then click the target for the command.

⑩ Click the Close buttons in open dialog boxes to finish the operation.

TIP: You can delete a switchboard page or an item by clicking it and then clicking the Delete button.

Documenting a Database

Keeping track of every table, query, and report in a database isn't that hard when the database is new and fresh in your memory, but as you add new objects and move on to other projects, it can be hard to remember everything about your database. You can have Access document the properties of selected objects in your database by running the Documenter. In the Documenter, you can choose the objects you want to get information about and then print a report, which gives you both a hard copy of your database in case something goes wrong and a report you can pass on to a programmer or administrator should you move on to other projects.

TRY THIS: Open the Northwind sample database, choose Analyze from the Tools menu, and then click Documenter. Click the All Object Types tab, click Deselect All, select the check box next to the Categories table, and then click OK. Click the body of the report that appears to view its contents. The report you just created contains detailed information about every object in your database.

Document a Database

1 Point to Analyze on the Tools menu, and then click Documenter.

2 Click the All Object Types tab.

3 Select or clear the check boxes to identify which elements of the database you want to document.

4 Click OK.

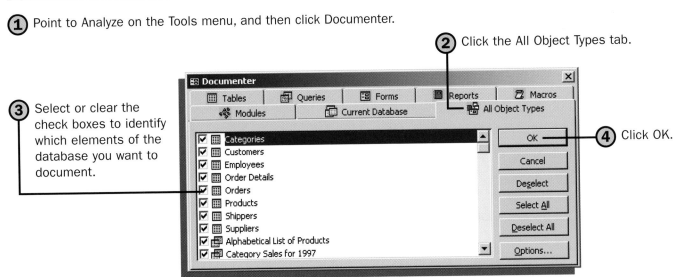

CAUTION: If you document every element of your database, the printed report could be extremely long.

Setting Startup Options

When you create a database for you and your colleagues to enter data, you might want to limit what your colleagues can do with the database. User permissions are one way to limit what your colleagues can do, but you can also hide the menu bars, the toolbars, and the database window so no one will be able to modify the database. When you create a database where users see only a designated form or report at startup, you've created an *application*. You won't want to do this with every database you create—only set these options for databases you know are in their final form and that you don't want to leave open to exploration by your colleagues.

Change an Application Title

1 Choose Startup from the Tools menu.

2 Type the name you want to appear on the title bar.

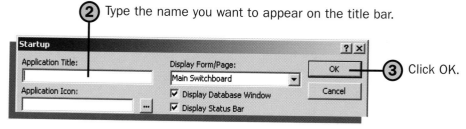

3 Click OK.

Hide All Menus

1 Choose Startup from the Tools menu.

2 Clear every check box in the Startup dialog box.

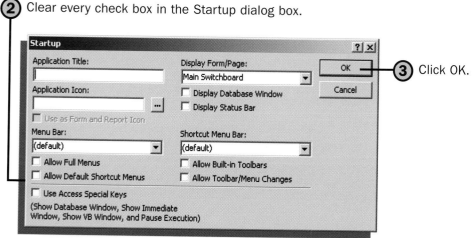

3 Click OK.

Set Startup Form or Page

① Choose Startup from the Tools menu.

② Click the Display Form/Page down arrow.

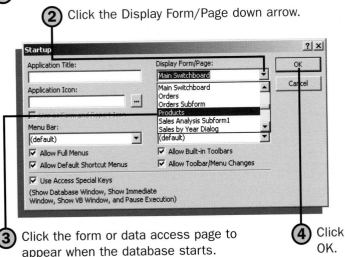

③ Click the form or data access page to appear when the database starts.

④ Click OK.

Set Startup Display Options

① Choose Options from the Tools menu.

② Click the View tab.

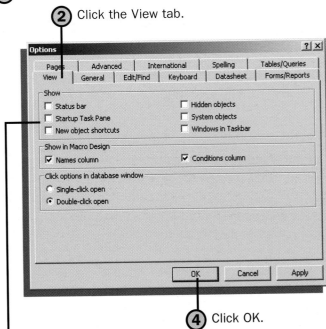

④ Click OK.

③ Clear every check box in the Show area of the dialog box to ensure that your database window will display nothing but the default form at startup.

CAUTION: Clicking (None) on the Display Form/Page drop-down list means no form or data access page will open when you or your colleagues run the database. If you hide the database window on startup, your colleagues won't be able to view the database's contents!

SEE ALSO: For information about limiting who can change your database, see "Creating User Accounts" on page 174.

14 Customizing Access

Microsoft Access is designed so you that can create and use your databases quickly and easily. As you get more familiar with the program, you may find that you perform some tasks more frequently than others or that you'd work more effectively if the toolbars or menus were set up a little differently. You can modify how Access presents itself to you to make your work flow quickly.

One way you can change the Access interface is to add or remove buttons from the Database toolbar. Clicking the Toolbar Options button, which is the small button at the far right edge of every toolbar, shows a list of all buttons available for that toolbar. If there are buttons you don't use, you can click them and hide them.

Finally, you can automate repetitive tasks by creating *macros*, or series of actions you can create and run whenever you need to.

In this chapter, you'll learn how to:

● Modify toolbars by adding, removing, and customizing buttons.

● Modify menus by adding, removing, and customizing items.

● Build a simple macro and either run it or step through it.

● Define macro groups and create macros with conditional steps.

● Use a macro to display a message box.

● Launch a macro when a command button is clicked.

Modifying Toolbars

When you install Microsoft Access, the toolbars and menus are set up so that the toolbar buttons you click to perform the most common tasks (such as saving your working or printing a copy of a database object) are easy to find. When you're just starting out with Access, it's a good idea to leave the screen in its original arrangement. Once you've worked with the program for a while, though, you may decide that a different arrangement of toolbar buttons would suit your work habits or perhaps even that you could hide a few toolbar buttons you never use to save space. In that case, you can change the toolbar's layout to meet your needs.

Add or Remove Toolbar Buttons

1 Click the Toolbar Options button on the toolbar where you want to add or remove buttons.

3 Point to the toolbar name. The actual menu item that appears reflects the name of the toolbar on which you clicked the Toolbar Options button.

2 Point to Add Or Remove Buttons.

4 Click the button you want to add or remove.

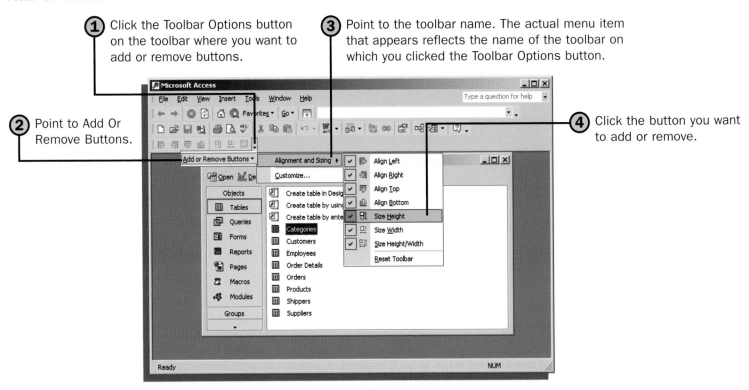

! **TIP:** You can change a toolbar back to its original configuration by clicking Reset Toolbar, which appears at the bottom of the list of available buttons.

Add Any Access Button to a Toolbar

① Choose Customize from the Tools menu.

② If necessary, click the Commands tab.

③ Click the category from which you want to drag the toolbar button.

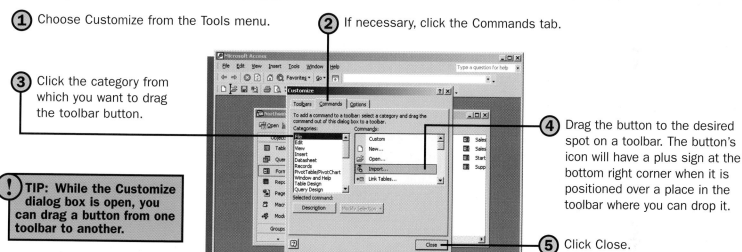

④ Drag the button to the desired spot on a toolbar. The button's icon will have a plus sign at the bottom right corner when it is positioned over a place in the toolbar where you can drop it.

⑤ Click Close.

! **TIP: While the Customize dialog box is open, you can drag a button from one toolbar to another.**

Edit a Toolbar Button

① Choose Customize from the Tools menu.

② Right-click the toolbar button you want to edit.

③ Point to Change Button Image on the shortcut menu that appears.

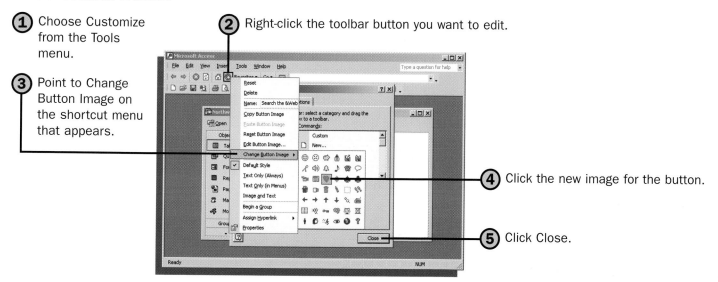

④ Click the new image for the button.

⑤ Click Close.

Modifying Menus

The menu system is similar to the toolbars and toolbar buttons. In fact, Access treats toolbars and menus the same "on the inside." In practical terms, that means clicking the Save toolbar button and choosing Save from the File menu are equivalent actions. So why have both systems in place? It's a matter of user preference. Some folks like to use toolbar buttons while others (your author included) prefer to use the menu system. And, just as you can customize toolbars to put everything where you want it, you can modify the layout of your menus to fit your work style.

Add an Item to a Menu

① Choose Customize from the Tools menu.

② If necessary, click the Commands tab.

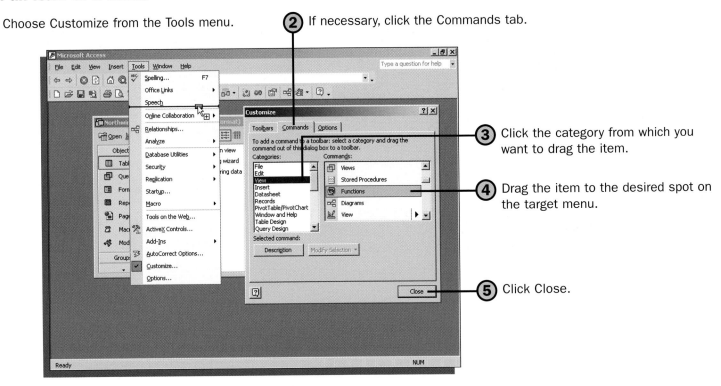

③ Click the category from which you want to drag the item.

④ Drag the item to the desired spot on the target menu.

⑤ Click Close.

Edit a Menu Item

① Choose Customize from the Tools menu.

② Click the menu containing the item you want to edit.

③ Right-click the menu item you want to edit.

④ Type a new name for the menu item, and then press Enter.

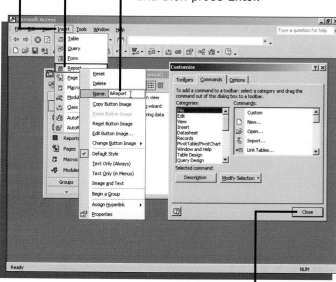

⑤ Click Close.

Delete a Menu Item

① Choose Customize from the Tools menu.

② Click the menu containing the item you want to delete.

③ Drag the item from the menu to the Customize dialog box.

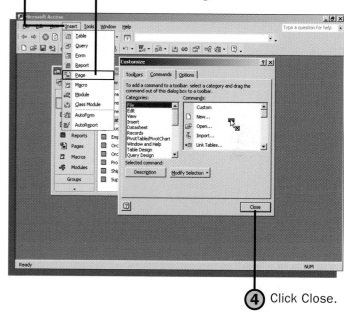

④ Click Close.

⚠ TIP: The letter preceded by the ampersand ("&") is the shortcut key for that menu item. For example, if you display the File menu, typing the letter o does the same thing as clicking the Open command. The shortcut key letter is underlined in the item's name; not every item has a shortcut key assigned to it.

Building a Macro

A *macro* is a series of automated steps, such as opening a report or a form or displaying a message box, that you create and save. After you save the macro, you can run it whenever you want, either by double-clicking it in the database window or by running it when something specific happens, such as clicking a button on a form. If you export Access tables to other formats, print records, or search for records and are tired of going through the process manually, you can create a macro that does it for you.

Create a Macro

1 Click Macros on the Objects bar.

2 Click New.

3 Click the down arrow in the first Action cell.

4 Click the action that you want as the first step in the macro.

7 Type a name for your macro.

8 Click OK.

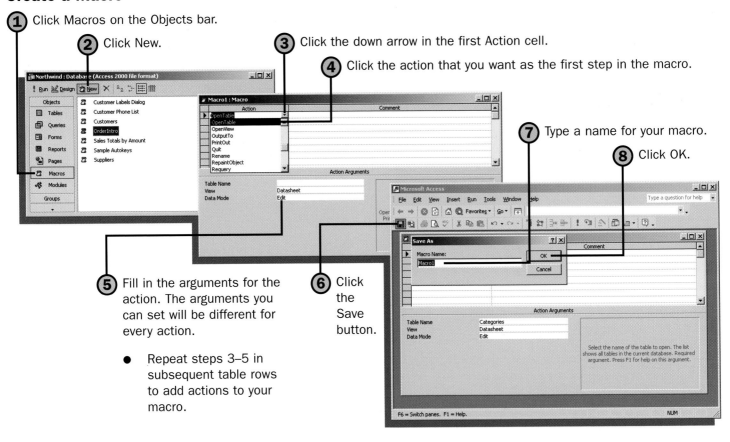

5 Fill in the arguments for the action. The arguments you can set will be different for every action.

- Repeat steps 3–5 in subsequent table rows to add actions to your macro.

6 Click the Save button.

Running a Macro

Once you've created a macro, you can run it (that is, have Access execute the macro's steps) several ways. The most straightforward way to run a macro is to display the macros in your database, click the one you want to run, and then click the Run button. If a macro doesn't do what you expect, or if you're just curious to see how it works, you can step through the macro one action at a time. While you're stepping through the macro, Access lets you know what's going on so that you can learn what the macro is doing and either fix a problem or apply what you've learned to macros you create on your own.

Run a Macro

① Click Macros on the Objects bar.

③ Click Run.   **②** Click the macro you want to run.

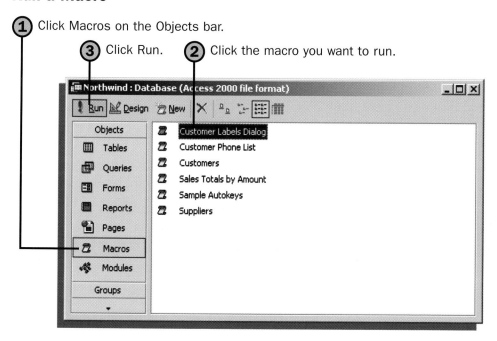

SEE ALSO: For more information about launching a macro when a form is opened, see "Running a Macro When a Form Opens" on page 200.

Step Through a Macro

1 Click Macros on the Objects bar.

3 Click Design. **2** Click the macro you want to step through.

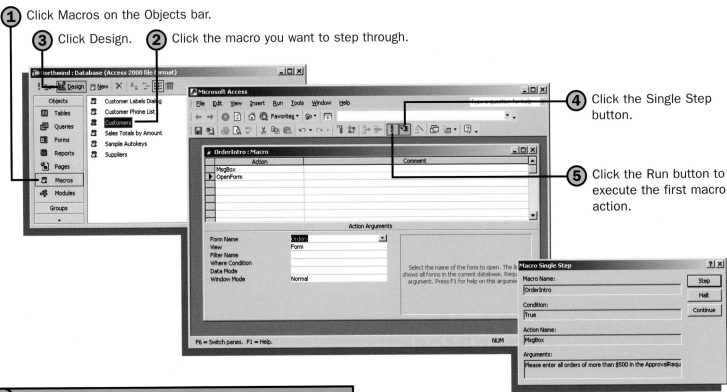

4 Click the Single Step button.

5 Click the Run button to execute the first macro action.

> ⚠ **TIP:** If you're working with a macro in a new database, taking the time to step through the macro can teach you a lot about the database and its structure.

> ✋ **CAUTION:** If the Single Step button is selected (outlined in blue), the macro will run in Single Step mode until you click the Single Step button again.

6 Follow any of these steps:

- Click Step to execute the next macro action.

- Click Halt to stop running the macro.

- Click Continue to run the macro without pausing between steps.

Defining Macro Groups

After you've gotten the hang of creating macros and have discovered how much time they can save you, you'll probably create lots of macros to print table contents, import data, or run searches. Managing dozens of macro files can take lots of time and energy, but there is an easier way! If you create a series of macros that are related by the objects they work on or the actions they perform, you can save the macros in a single file and identify individual macros by their name. In a way, defining a macro group is like having a bunch of files in a directory—when the macros are grouped by theme, or by the name of the form from which they're run, they're that much easier to find.

Create a Macro Group

1 Click Macros on the Objects bar.

2 Click the macro file in which you want to save a group of macros.

3 Click Design.

5 Type the name for the first macro.

6 Click the second cell in the Action column.

4 Click the Macro Names button.

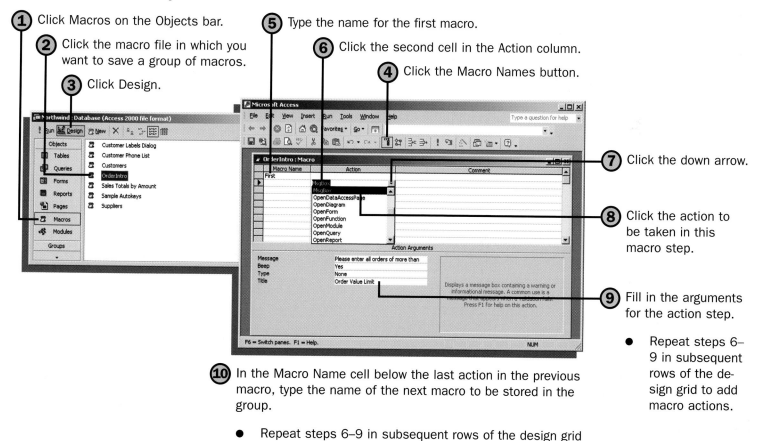

7 Click the down arrow.

8 Click the action to be taken in this macro step.

9 Fill in the arguments for the action step.

- Repeat steps 6–9 in subsequent rows of the design grid to add macro actions.

10 In the Macro Name cell below the last action in the previous macro, type the name of the next macro to be stored in the group.

- Repeat steps 6–9 in subsequent rows of the design grid to add actions to the second macro.

Building Conditional Macros

When you create a macro, you'll usually want Access to perform every action whenever the macro is run. Sometimes, though, you'll only want Access to take certain actions when particular conditions are true. You might only want the macro to print records representing orders with values over $500, for example, or to print every record for customers who haven't placed an order in the last month. In either case, you can set conditions to govern which actions are taken.

Create a Conditional Macro

(1) Click Macros on the Objects bar.

(3) Click Design. (2) Click the macro in which you want to make a step conditional.

(5) Click the Condition cell next to the action you want to make conditional.

(4) Click the Conditions button.

(6) Click the Build button.

(7) Create the condition in the Expression Builder.

(8) Click OK.

(9) Click the Save button on the Macro Design toolbar.

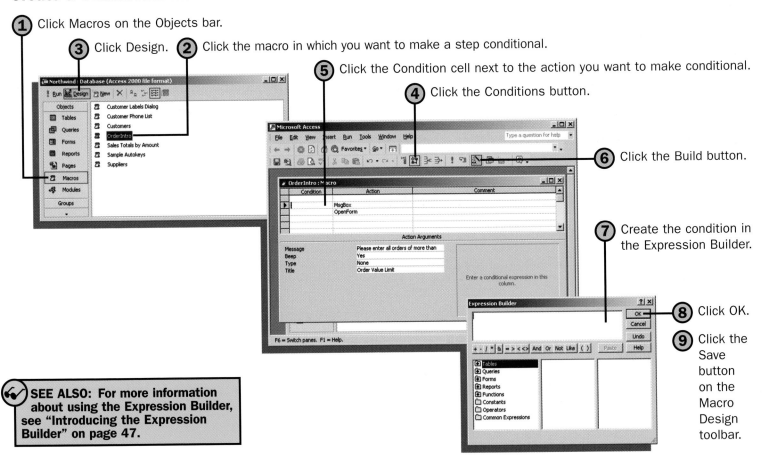

SEE ALSO: For more information about using the Expression Builder, see "Introducing the Expression Builder" on page 47.

Adding and Deleting Macro Actions

Macros are a great way to do whatever you want with Access, but there may be times when you want to extend a macro's capabilities. Perhaps you forgot to open a form in your macro, want to open a new form you just created, or just want to add a blank line to the design grid so that your macro is easier to read. To add a blank line to a macro, all you need to do is click the Insert Rows button. By the same token, you can remove an existing action, or blank line, from a macro by clicking the Delete Rows button. None of your changes are finalized until you save the macro, so if anything goes wrong you can close the macro without saving your changes.

Insert a Macro Step

1 Click Macros on the Objects bar.

2 Click the macro into which you want to insert a step.

3 Click Design.

4 Click any cell in the row below where you want the new row to appear.

5 Click the Insert Rows button.

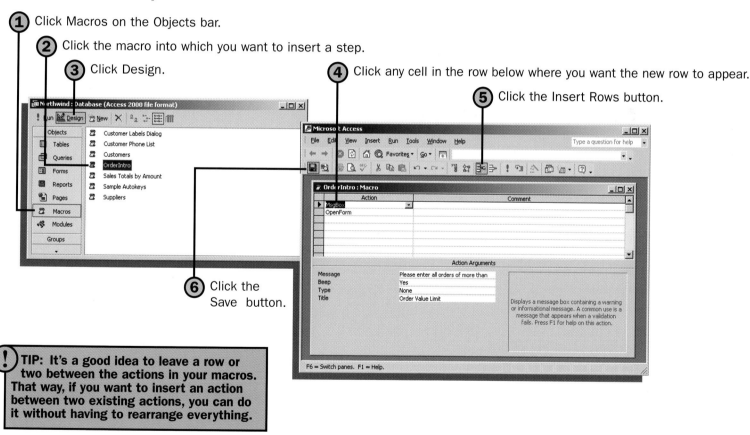

6 Click the Save button.

> **TIP:** It's a good idea to leave a row or two between the actions in your macros. That way, if you want to insert an action between two existing actions, you can do it without having to rearrange everything.

Delete a Macro Step

① Click Macros on the Objects bar.

② Click the macro from which you want to delete a step.

③ Click Design.

④ Click any cell in the row with the step you want to delete.

⑥ Click the Save button.

⑤ Click the Delete Rows button.

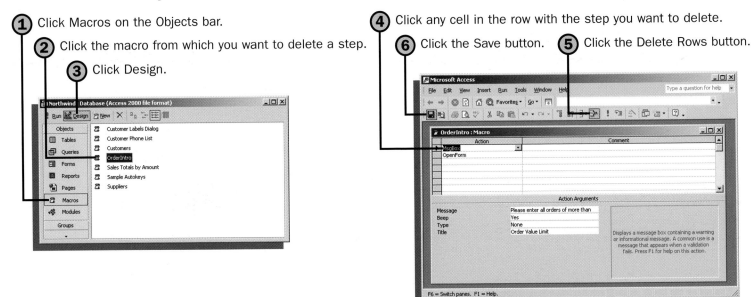

> **⚠ TIP:** If you're having trouble with a macro and want Access to skip a step, you don't have to delete the step and re-create it later. Instead just click the Conditions button to display the Condition column, and type False in the Condition cell of the step you want to skip. When you're ready to run the step again, just erase the word False and you're set!

Displaying a Message Box

One useful thing you can do with macros is to display a message box indicating what folks should expect to see while using your database. Your message box can have a message of up to 255 characters, giving you plenty of room to explain what sort of data to enter into a field, to give your colleague advice on the purpose of a form, or to indicate the last time a form was modified. If you want, you can have Access run a macro whenever someone opens a form. To do that, you set the form's On Open property, which offers a list of available macros.

Create a Message Box

① Click Macros on the Objects bar.

② Click New.

③ Click the first cell in the Action column.

④ Click the down arrow.

⑤ Click MsgBox.

⑥ Type the text to appear in the Message box.

⑦ Click Type.

⑧ Click the down arrow.

⑨ Click the type of message box you want to appear.

⑪ Click the Save button.

⑫ Type a name for the macro.

⑬ Click OK.

⑩ Type the text to appear on the title bar of the message box.

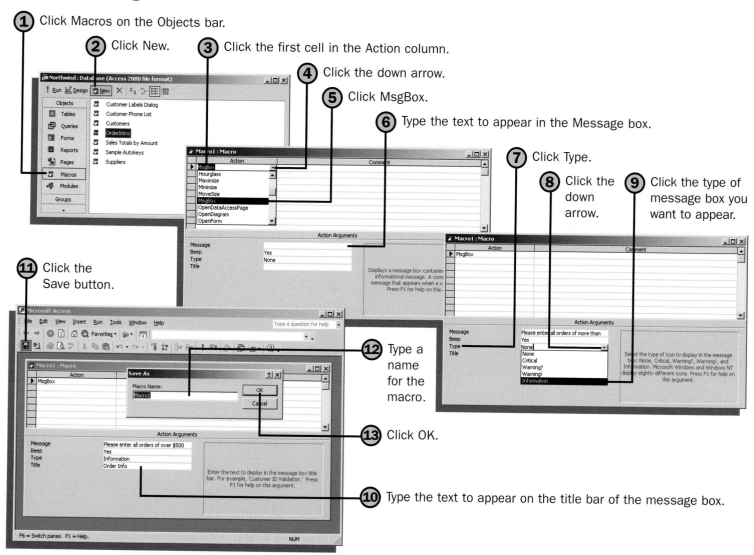

Launching a Macro from a Button

You and your colleagues can run any macro any time you want by double-clicking it in the main database window, but there is a better way to let your colleagues run a macro whenever they want. To do that, you can create a command button on a form and tell Access to run the macro whenever someone clicks the button. The Main Switchboard form that appears when you open the Northwind sample database has several such buttons that let you print sales reports or open the main database window.

Assign a Macro to a Button

① Open a form in Design view.

② If necessary, click the Toolbox button.

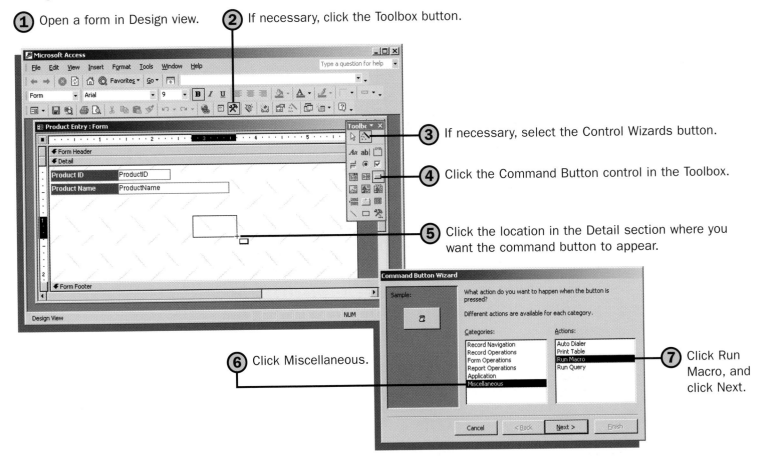

③ If necessary, select the Control Wizards button.

④ Click the Command Button control in the Toolbox.

⑤ Click the location in the Detail section where you want the command button to appear.

⑥ Click Miscellaneous.

⑦ Click Run Macro, and click Next.

8 Click the macro you want to run when the command button is clicked, and click Next.

9 Select the Text option.

10 Type the text to appear on the command button's face, and click Next.

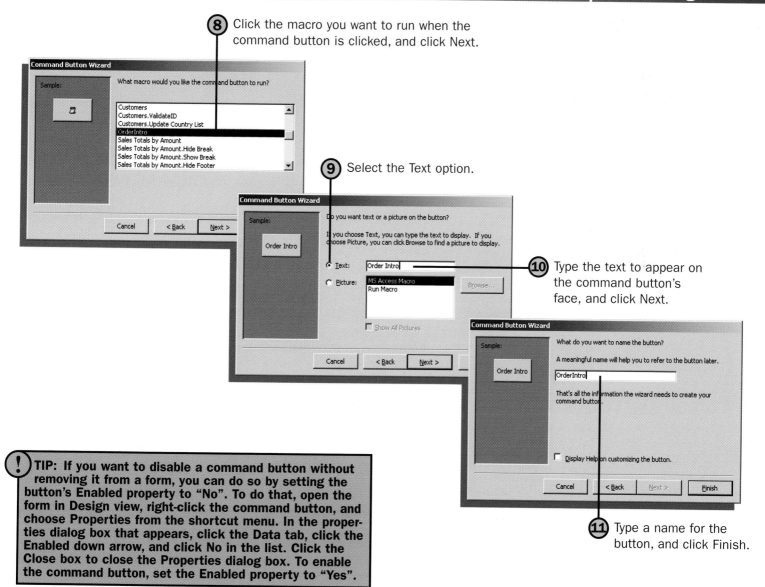

11 Type a name for the button, and click Finish.

! **TIP:** If you want to disable a command button without removing it from a form, you can do so by setting the button's Enabled property to "No". To do that, open the form in Design view, right-click the command button, and choose Properties from the shortcut menu. In the properties dialog box that appears, click the Data tab, click the Enabled down arrow, and click No in the list. Click the Close box to close the Properties dialog box. To enable the command button, set the Enabled property to "Yes".

Running a Macro When a Form Opens

The best form designs put as much data as possible on the page, but it's also important that the data be readable. After all, if you cram every field together on a form, you might as well display the data as a datasheet! One way you can give you and your colleagues information about how a form works without taking up any of your form's "real estate" is to display a message box when the form opens. By having the message box appear at the start, you ensure that your message is seen without getting in the way of the data on the form.

SEE ALSO: For more information about creating a macro that displays a message box, see "Displaying a Message Box" on page 196.

Run a Macro When a Form Opens

① Open a form in Design view.

② Double-click the Form Selector.

③ Click the Event tab.

④ Click On Open.

⑤ Click the down arrow.

⑥ Click the macro you want to run when the form opens.

⑦ Click the Close box.

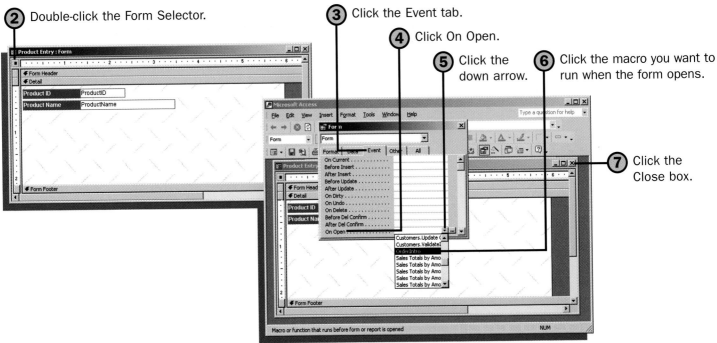

Preventing Toolbar Modifications

When you've found a comfortable working setup for the toolbars and menu bars in Access, you might want to change your Access options so that anyone exploring the program's menu and toolbar system won't be able to delete any menu items or toolbar buttons without changing this setting as well. Even if you think the risk of someone finding their way into the Customize dialog box and undoing your hard work is remote, you should still consider preventing any toolbar or menu changes to ensure your database works as planned.

SEE ALSO: For information about hiding the menu bar and toolbars, see "Setting Startup Options" on page 183.

Protect Toolbars and Menus from Changes

1 Choose Startup from the Tools menu.

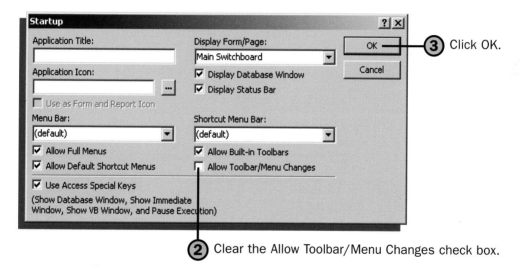

3 Click OK.

2 Clear the Allow Toolbar/Menu Changes check box.

Extending the Recently Used File List

When you install Access, the last four databases you opened appear near the bottom of the File menu. To open one of the listed files, all you need to do is click its name. If you work with a lot of databases, however, you may find that four names isn't enough to maintain a list of your frequently-used databases. Rather than go digging through your directories to find your databases, you can extend the Recently Used File List to display the names of up to nine databases. If you set the number of files to zero, the file names won't appear on the File menu, but they won't be forgotten, either. Changing the value to a number greater than zero will still display the last several files you opened.

Display Recently Used Files

1 Choose Options from the Tools menu.

2 Click the General tab.

TIP: If you rename or move a database, its listing on the Recently Used File List will no longer work.

3 Select the Recently Used File List check box.

4 Click the down arrow.

5 Click the number of files to display. Clicking 0 or clearing the Recently Used File List check box both have the effect of displaying no files in the list.

6 Click OK.

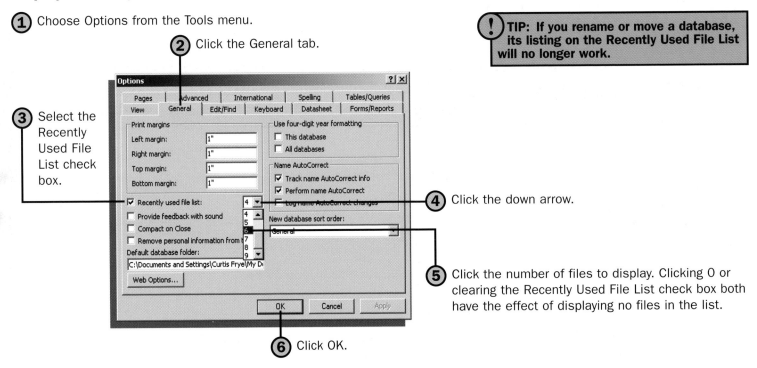

15 Presenting Table and Query Data Dynamically

The capabilities Access places at your disposal are wide-ranging and powerful. You can build tables to store data effectively, ask questions of the data using queries, and display the data in forms and reports. What's even better, you can use many of those techniques in a single database object: the PivotTable Report.

When you create a PivotTable, you build a versatile object you can use as part of live business presentations to illustrate your own points and answer your colleagues' questions quickly. If you'd rather summarize your data visually, you can create PivotChart Reports, which let you reorganize and redisplay your data in a chart.

In this section, you'll learn how to:

● Create a PivotTable.

● Dynamically reorganize the data in your PivotTable.

● Filter the values that appear on a PivotTable.

● Format a PivotTable.

● Create a PivotChart.

● Change a PivotChart's chart type.

Introducing PivotTables and PivotCharts

One of the strengths of Microsoft Access is the flexibility you have in choosing how to present your data. The most basic method of presenting your data is in a table, where the data is listed one row at a time. Displaying your data in a form lets you present the data one record at a time; reports give you the additional ability to organize your table contents or query results based on grouping levels. Finally, if one field in your table or query is related to two other fields in the table or query, such as with sales data for the quantity of a given product sold in a month, you can create a crosstab query to present the data in relation to the other fields.

PivotTables let you combine all of these abilities into a single database object, with some added benefits thrown in. Not only can you present your data in an easily understood format, you can also change the data's organization while you have the PivotTable open. As with other database objects, Access steps you through the PivotTable creation process with a wizard that explains everything you need to do.

Pivoting

When you open a form that contains a PivotTable, you'll see your data in a layout that is similar to that of a crosstab query.

Field head   Field head   Field head

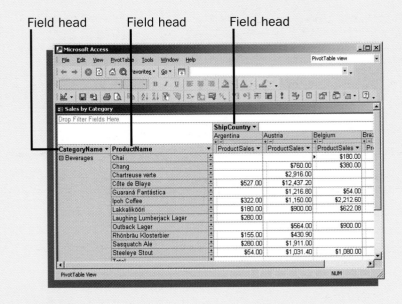

The added value in using PivotTables is that you can reorganize the data in the PivotTable by moving the field heads to reflect the desired layout (as shown in the first graphic on the facing page).

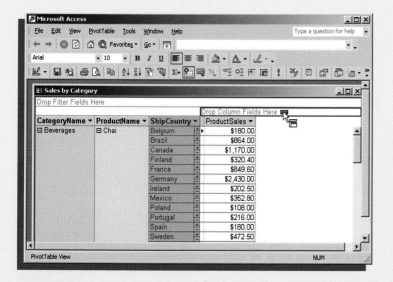

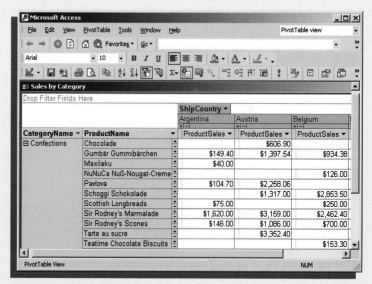

Once you choose the values you want to concentrate on, clicking OK limits the contents of the PivotTable to the items you selected.

Filtering

When you work with large data collections, it's important that you be able to limit the data that appears on the screen. With PivotTables, you can click the down arrow at the right edge of a field head and choose the values to display.

PivotCharts

Just as you can create PivotTables, which let you reorganize your table data, you can create PivotCharts to summarize your data graphically. As with a PivotTable, you can change how the PivotChart presents your data, both by reorganizing the data and by changing the PivotChart's chart type.

Creating a PivotTable

Access databases let you gather and present important data, but the standard table only shows a list of values. Forms and reports let you summarize and display your data so that it's easier to evaluate, but you're still limited to a single view of your data. Even queries, which let you perform calculations on your data or present it in a crosstab worksheet, give you a single view of your data. PivotTables, by contrast, let you rearrange your data dynamically. If your PivotTable lists sales by category and you'd rather see the data organized by country, you can change the layout of your PivotTable quickly. Once you create your first PivotTable, you'll understand how powerful a tool they are!

Step Through the PivotTable Wizard

SEE ALSO: For information about using the Drop Filter Fields Here area, see "Filtering PivotTable Data" on page 211.

TIP: Adding every field from the table or query you're using to create your PivotTable is the best way to go. You won't need to use all of the fields in the PivotTable, but they'll be available if you do want them.

① Click Forms on the Objects bar, and then click New.

② Click PivotTable Wizard.

③ Click the down arrow.

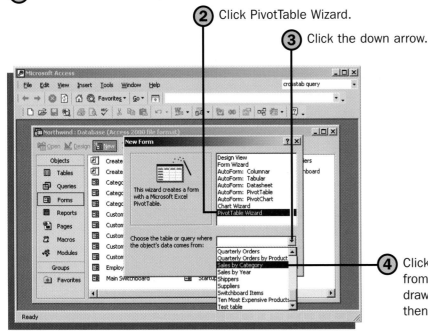

④ Click the table or query from which you want to draw your data, and then click OK.

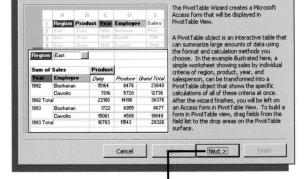

⑤ Click Next to clear the information screen that appears.

> **TIP:** When you create a PivotTable, you should make sure "PivotTable" appears in the name of the form you created. It doesn't change how the form operates, but it does make it easier to find.

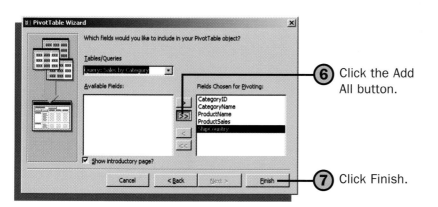

6 Click the Add All button.

7 Click Finish.

8 Drag fields that you want to provide values for in the PivotTable's rows from the PivotTable Field List dialog box to the Drop Row Fields Here area.

9 Drag fields that you want to provide values for in the PivotTable's columns from the PivotTable Field List dialog box to the Drop Column Fields Here area.

PivotTable Field List dialog box

10 Drag the fields that you want to provide values for the body of the PivotTable from the PivotTable Field List dialog box to the Drop Totals Or Detail Fields Here area.

Adding and Removing PivotTable Fields

After you create a PivotTable, you can arrange the fields on the PivotTable to present your data effectively. It is possible your colleagues could ask questions you'd hadn't thought of, but that you could answer if you included another field in the PivotTable and used it to filter or organize your data. Maybe they're interested in how dairy products have been selling in South America. While you didn't include the countries for each sale in the original PivotTable design, that data is in the query you based the PivotTable on. All you need to do is add it to the design. By the same token, you can remove any fields you're not using. You can drag them from the body of the PivotTable to the field list box, ready for use if you need them again.

Add a Field to a PivotTable

1 Click Forms on the Objects bar.

2 Click the form containing the PivotTable.

3 Click Design.

4 If necessary, click the Field List button.

6 Choose PivotTable View from the View menu.

8 Drag the new field to the desired spot on the PivotTable.

7 Click the Field List button.

5 Drag the field you want to add to the Detail section of the form.

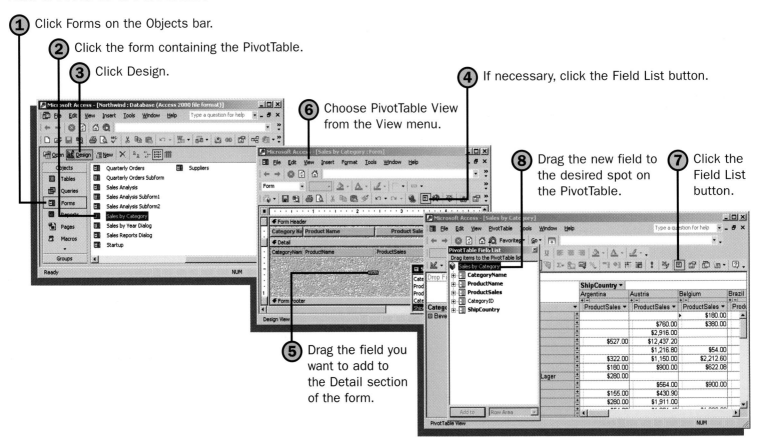

Remove a Field from a PivotTable

① Click Forms on the Objects bar.

③ Click Open.

② Click the form containing the PivotTable.

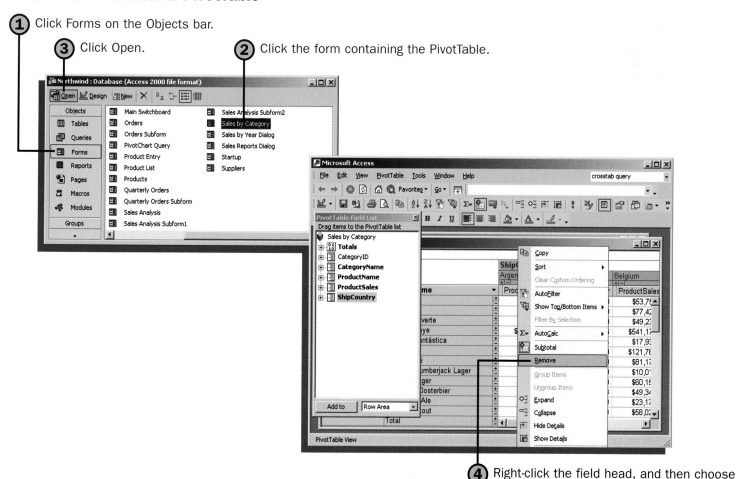

④ Right-click the field head, and then choose Remove from the shortcut menu.

> **⚠ TIP: If you want to add a field to the PivotTable and the field already appears in the PivotTable Field List dialog box, you can just drag the field to the desired spot on the layout.**

Pivoting a PivotTable

Perhaps the biggest benefit of presenting your data using PivotTables is that you can change the data's organization on the fly, creating literally dozens of different worksheets from a single data set! All you have to do is drag the header of the field you want to move to its new position—when you release the mouse button, Access will examine the PivotTable's new structure and rearrange the data to match it. If previously you had listed sales by Country and then by product Category, you could drag the Category field header to the left of the Country field header to reverse the grouping.

Reorganize PivotTable Data

1 Click Forms on the Objects bar.

3 Click Open.

2 Click the Form containing the PivotTable you want to open.

4 Drag the header you want to relocate to the desired position on the PivotTable.

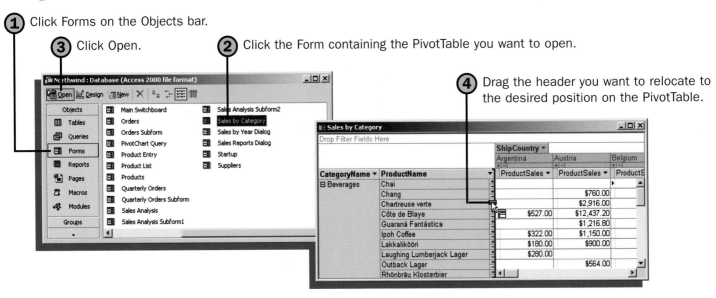

TIP: If you use a lot of fields in your PivotTable, you might not be able to remember the exact ordering of fields that produced a particular arrangement. When you find an arrangement that presents your data effectively, you should send yourself an e-mail message with the order or record the arrangement in a Word document so that you can re-create the arrangement quickly.

Filtering PivotTable Data

When you create a PivotTable from the data in your tables or queries, you will often have several screens worth of data to move through. Reorganizing your data can help you interpret your data, but you can also filter your PivotTable by choosing the data you want to see. For example, if your PivotTable shows sales data for a series of products grouped by category, you can pick the categories for which you want to view data.

Select Which Field Values to Display

1 Click Forms on the Objects bar.

3 Click Open. **2** Click the form containing the PivotTable.

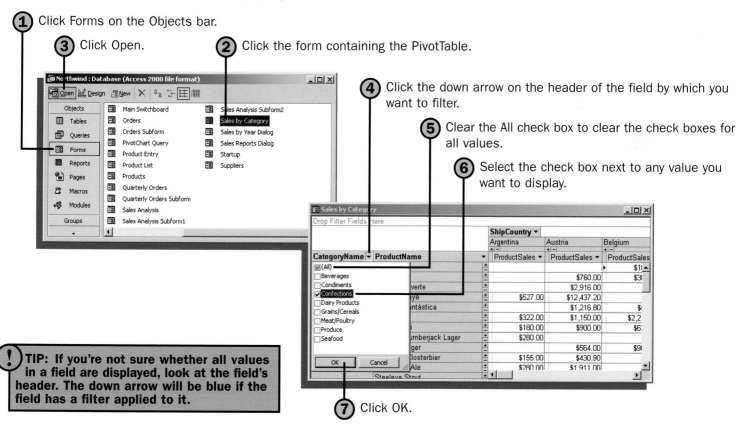

4 Click the down arrow on the header of the field by which you want to filter.

5 Clear the All check box to clear the check boxes for all values.

6 Select the check box next to any value you want to display.

TIP: If you're not sure whether all values in a field are displayed, look at the field's header. The down arrow will be blue if the field has a filter applied to it.

7 Click OK.

Filter by a Field Not Displayed in the Body of a PivotTable

① Click Forms on the Objects bar.

③ Click Open.

② Click the form containing the PivotTable you want to filter.

④ Click the Field List button.

⑤ Drag the field by which you want to filter the PivotTable to the Drop Filter Fields Here area.

⑥ Click the down arrow on the field header.

⑦ Clear the All check box.

⑨ Click OK.

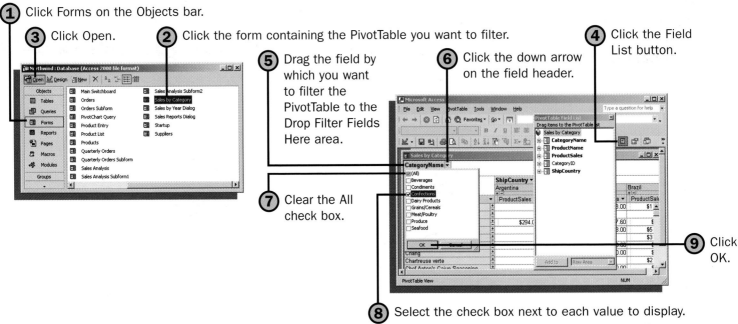

⑧ Select the check box next to each value to display.

Toggle a Filter On and Off

① Click the AutoFilter button to remove a filter.

② Click the AutoFilter button again to reapply the filter.

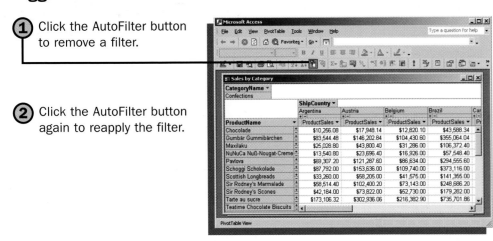

Formatting a PivotTable

PivotTables are all about presenting your data effectively, and a significant element of any presentation is the appearance of your data. To change the appearance of an element of your PivotTable, such as the color, pattern, and font, use the Properties dialog box.

Change a PivotTable's Appearance

1 Click Forms on the Objects bar.

3 Click Open.

2 Click the Form containing the PivotTable you want to format.

4 Click the part of the Pivot-Table you want to format.

5 Click the Properties button.

7 Click the Close box.

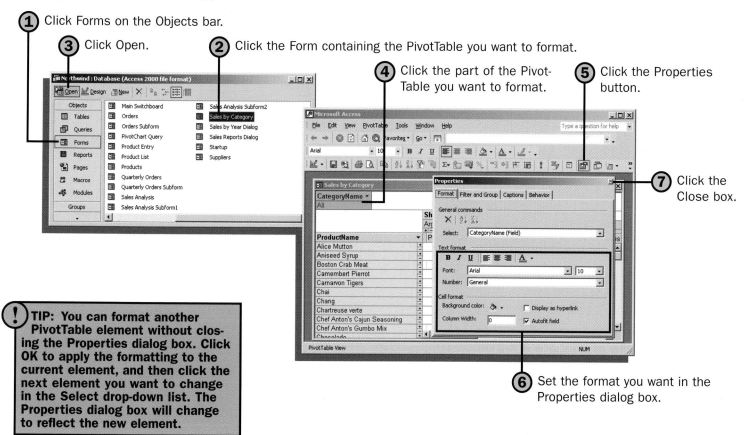

6 Set the format you want in the Properties dialog box.

> **TIP:** You can format another PivotTable element without closing the Properties dialog box. Click OK to apply the formatting to the current element, and then click the next element you want to change in the Select drop-down list. The Properties dialog box will change to reflect the new element.

 CAUTION: Any changes you make in Design view, including applying an AutoFormat, won't appear in PivotTable view.

Creating a PivotChart

Just as you can create tables that you can reorganize on the fly to emphasize different aspects of your table and query data, you can also create dynamic charts, or PivotCharts, to summarize your data effectively. By changing the grouping order of the fields used to create your PivotChart, or by limiting which values are presented in the PivotChart, you answer specific questions posed by you and your colleagues. In addition to letting you change how your data appears in the chart, you can even change the type of chart you use to display your data!

Step Through the PivotChart Wizard

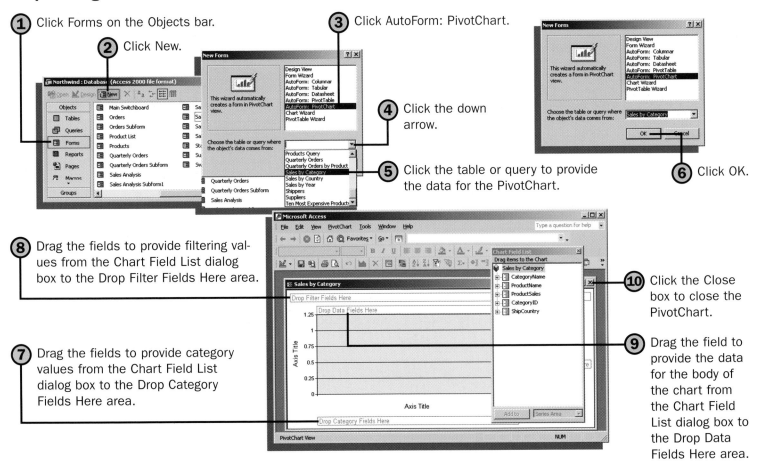

1 Click Forms on the Objects bar.

2 Click New.

3 Click AutoForm: PivotChart.

4 Click the down arrow.

5 Click the table or query to provide the data for the PivotChart.

6 Click OK.

7 Drag the fields to provide category values from the Chart Field List dialog box to the Drop Category Fields Here area.

8 Drag the fields to provide filtering values from the Chart Field List dialog box to the Drop Filter Fields Here area.

9 Drag the field to provide the data for the body of the chart from the Chart Field List dialog box to the Drop Data Fields Here area.

10 Click the Close box to close the PivotChart.

Change a PivotChart Chart Type

(1) Click Forms on the Objects bar.

(3) Click Open.

(2) Click the form containing the PivotChart.

(4) Click the Chart Type button on the PivotChart toolbar.

(5) Click the Type tab.

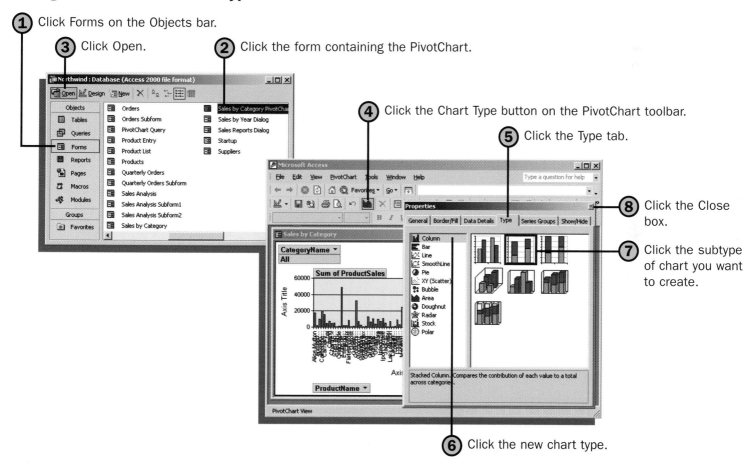

(8) Click the Close box.

(7) Click the subtype of chart you want to create.

(6) Click the new chart type.

Index

Send feedback about this index to
mspindex@microsoft.com

sample databases, 20
saving
  forms, 23
  objects, 21
  objects as Web pages, 160
  Save button and, 157, 188, 190, 194
  tables as XML documents, 167
scrambling information, 171
Search task pane, 8–9
sections, report, 110
security, 169–76
select queries, 82
shapes, 127–28
shortcut
  keys, 122, 189
  menu, 61–62, 187, 209
shortcuts, desktop, 10
showing. *See* hiding and showing
shutdown, 2, 14
single pages, printing, 16
sites, Web, 156
sizing. *See* resizing
sorting. *See* grouping
special effects, 123
spelling errors, 58
spreadsheets, exporting data and, 153
startup
  creating shortcut for, 10
  opening databases on, 12
  setting options, 183–84
  with Start button, 9, 164
Status bar, 11
storage, data, 6–7. *See also* data; databases
strings, zero-length, 50

style
  data access page, 165
  Form Wizard and, 70
  report and display, 27
  themes and, 165
subdatasheets, 63–64
subforms, 69, 77–79, 113
subreports, 77, 99, 112–13
summary reports, 102–3
Switchboard Manager, 180–81
switchboards, 19, 24, 169, 180–81
system clipboard, 8

tables, 7, 55–68
  Autocorrect and, 58–59
  charts and, 150
  columns, 22, 61–63 (*see also* fields)
  creating, 35–36
  data access pages and, 160–61
  data entry and, 58–59
  Datasheet view and, 55
  documenting, 182
  exporting data, 153
  filtering PivotTable data, 211
  filtering records, 65–68
  forms and, 23 (*see also* forms)
  hyperlinks and, 157
  importing data, 38, 152
  inserting objects, 145
  locking database records, 176
  macros and, 190
  objects and, 32
  PivotCharts and PivotTables and, 204, 214
  primary and foreign keys for, 33, 37 (*see also* primary key fields)

tables, *continued*
  queries and reports and, 25, 85–86, 94, 100
    (*see also* queries; reports)
  referential integrity and, 41
  relationships between, 39–40
  rows, 62–63 (*see also* records)
  subdatasheets, 55, 63–64
  subforms and, 78
  text, 56–57, 59–60
  User-Level Security Wizard and, 174
  viewing and navigating, 22
  Word, 6–7
  XML and, 167
Tabular AutoReports, 104
tags, HTML, 156
targets, switchboard, 181
task panes, 8–9, 11–12, 34
technical language, 1–2
templates, 26, 48–49
text
  adding, with AutoCorrect, 58–59
  adding and editing, 59–60
  conditional formatting and, 132
  finding and replacing, 56–57
  formatting, 118
  query criteria and, 87
  tags, 156
  zero-length strings, 50
themes, 164–65
tiling, 136
title bar
  Access Window, 11
  maximizing windows with, 13
  task pane, 9
toolbars
  Database, 11
  Formatting, 118, 122

About the Author

Curtis Frye is a freelance writer based in Portland, Oregon. *Microsoft Access Version 2002 Plain & Simple* is his second solo book for Microsoft Press; he also wrote *Microsoft Excel Version 2002 Step by Step* and co-authored both *Microsoft Excel Version 2002 Plain & Simple* and *Microsoft Office XP Step by Step*. For other publishers, he has written five books and online courses covering Microsoft technologies, plus an online course on advanced database design. On the academic front, he is the author of *Privacy-Enhanced Business*, was the lead author of O'Reilly & Associates' market research report "The State of Web Commerce," and is the editor and chief reviewer of *Technology and Society Book Reviews*. Originally from Mt. Crawford, Virginia, Curt received his political science degree from Syracuse University in 1990. While a member of the technical staff at The MITRE Corporation in McLean, Virginia, he attended graduate school in information systems at George Mason University. When not busy writing, and often when he is busy writing, he is a professional improvisational comedian with ComedySportz Portland.

The manuscript for this book was prepared and submitted to Microsoft Press in electronic form. Text files were prepared using Microsoft Word 2002. Pages were composed by Microsoft Press using Adobe PageMaker 6.52 for Windows, with text set in Times and display type in ITC Franklin Gothic. Composed pages were delivered to the printer as electronic prepress files.

Cover Graphic Designer

Tim Girvin Design

Interior Graphic Designers

Joel Panchot, James D. Kramer

Interior Graphic Artists

Rob Nance, Paula Gorelick

Principal Compositor

Paula Gorelick

Principal Proofreader/Copy Editor

Lisa Pawlewicz

Indexer

Shane-Armstrong Information Systems

7975 278

ROWAN UNIVERSITY CAMPBELL LIBRARY

3 3001 00905 253 0

QA 76.9 .D3 F793 20

1

Frye, Curtis, 1968-
Microsoft Access version
2002 plain & simple

DATE DUE

GAYLORD | No. 2333 | | PRINTED IN U.S.A.